How to Dress Dancers
Costuming Techniques for Dance

Mary Kent Harrison

A DANCE HORIZONS BOOK

Princeton Book Company,
Publishers
Princeton, New Jersey

1988, Princeton Book Company, Publishers
© 1975, 1978, Midas Books Ltd.

A Dance Horizons Book
Princeton Book Company, Publishers
POB 57
Pennington, NJ 08534

ISBN 0-916622-72-X   (cloth)
ISBN 0-916622-73-8   (paper)

LC# 88-60948

Cover Design by Main Street Design

Contents

List of Plates

Plate 1.   Mid European Costume

FOREWORD

Making a costume from a sketch or illustration is a bewildering task. Especially if its purpose is for dancing, with all its exactitudes and limitations. How does one start? Where to begin? What about materials, and colour effects?

The following notes and diagrams are intended as a simple guide.

Many excellent books are available giving information of the actual costumes, from history and from folk traditions of countries and peoples. It is not my intention to add to these. However, the purpose of these notes is to show how the sketches can be "translated" into the actual garment. The few costume designs are included as examples only.

Dancing imposes limitations on costume designs and construction, which do not occur in those for the actor's stage. Fabrics must be specially light, so that they flow and move well, and length must be adjusted to suit the choreographer's requirements, rather than too rigid accuracy. Costumes for dancing must give the *illusion* of the real garment, and not become a meticulous reproduction. Emphasis is laid on simplicity, and an avoidance of irrelevant detail. At the same time a perfect fit must be obtained so that the line of the body beneath the costume is never lost.

In National and Character costumes where rich design and embroidery is called for, simple ways of giving effect are explained. Small detail should give way to a simplified decorative design. From the auditorium, minute detail is invisible.

In abstract and modern work, often a mere suggestion or hint of the theme is all that should be incorporated, leaving as much as possible to the imagination.

Technically, sewing for dance costumes should be very strong, as much stress is caused by the movement, especially on darts and seams, which must give as close a fit as possible. Details such as oversewing of seams, and some lining finishings are not worth carrying out. However, care must be taken to avoid untidiness — frayed edges, bad fastenings, uneven hem lines etc. These catch the eye and are distracting to the audience, and can ruin the whole effect of the costume.

A good head-dress can "make" a costume, and extra care should be taken over this, and also the choice of neatness of

hairstyle, underwear, hosiery, and of course shoes. A good
peticoat for National or Character costume is as important as
the over skirt which it supports.

Costumes for male dancers must be made with equal care
and regard for good simple line. A tailored effect is even more
necessary here, despite the fact that the fabrics must be light
in weight and supple enough to allow for free movement.

The importance of perfectly fitting leotard and tights for
the male dancer cannot be over-emphasised. No crease or edge
of underwear must appear beneath to break the line. Over-
garments such as classical tunics must have a glove-like fit,
and more elaborate costumes for period or national work must
be carefully made to fit each individual dancer. Nothing looks
worse than an ill-fitting jacket or cape on a male member of
the company, yet this is often where insufficient attention is
given.

Finally a word about colour. This sensitive question is one
for the designers, and great care should be taken to adhere
faithfully to his directives. No matter if the quality of the
material is cheap, as long as the colours are as required, and
the fabric is light enough to flow and "dance". Remember that
a delicate subtle colour arrangement is as important in some
settings as a rich and violent one can be in others. Colour
provides mood, feeling, atmosphere, sense of period, and
accuracy in National tradition. In modern work it should
enhance the musical mood.

The following notes are meant to *help*.

M.K.H.

LEOTARD

This is an important basic garment, upon which almost all dance costumes are founded.

First take careful measurements —

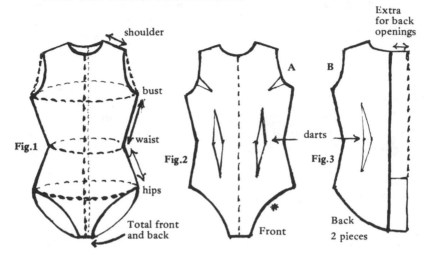

Plot out these measurements on paper, front and back, making the waist wider than necessary, so that a good fit can be achieved by darting, as in A and B above.

Using the paper as a pattern, cut out shapes in rough material such as old cotton sheeting, leaving ample margins for turnings.

Pin front and back together, and centre back below hip level. Fit carefully with pins, making sure the leg hole is not cut too high at the back, although the sides are cut up to hip-bone level, and fronts to groin crease, as at Fig. 1, 2*, 3 above.

Mark carefully all along the pin lines with pencil or tailor's chalk. If extensive adjustments have been made, correct the paper pattern accordingly, and KEEP it carefully as it is now a valuable basic pattern, specially for modern work, also for most National and Character bodices.

Seam sides, darts, shoulders and crutch seam. Face neck, arm-holes, and leg-holes. Fasten back opening with hooks and eyes. This leotard can be covered with any required fabric. Use the two materials together and cut and seam, as above, as one fabric.

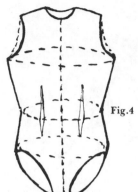

Fig.4

Pattern for male leotard will be less waisted, but will still need small dart at front and back.

Fasten on shoulders if fabric does not "give" sufficiently to be pulled up. No centre back opening.

The leotard is also the basic garment for all practice work.

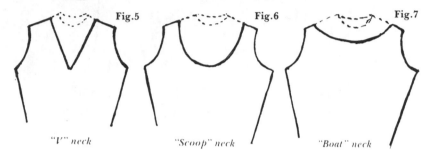

Fig.5   Fig.6   Fig.7

"V" neck   "Scoop" neck   "Boat" neck

Variations of neckline such as "V", "Scoop", "Boat", etc., can be substituted as desired in both male and female leotards.

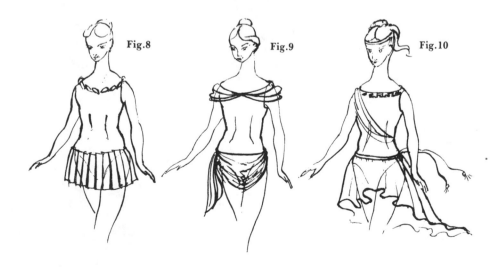

Fig.8   Fig.9   Fig.10

Fig.11

Fig.12

Fig.13

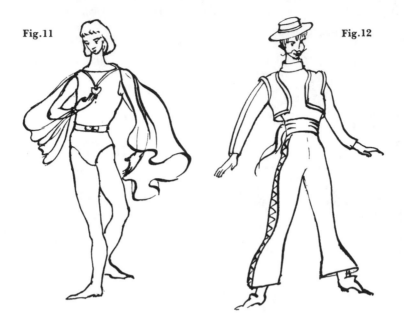

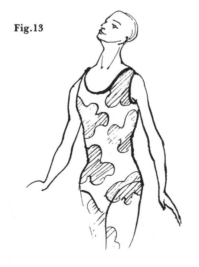

Plate 2. Persian Costume

BODICES

For Character or National Costumes.

Using the basic leotard pattern, cut the front and two backs in cotton (old sheet will do) and fit them with pins. Adjust pins to fit exactly.

 Fig.14

 Fig.15

See that the underarm seams are as high as possible under the arms.

Mark the pin lines with pencil, and take the three pieces apart. Using these as patterns, place and pin them over the required fabric (marked side showing), and cut out, round them. The two fabrics are now treated as one.

Decorations. These are added to the front and back at this stage, before side and shoulder seams are joined, on *right* side. Rejoin the seams on the marked pin lines.

Example. Corsage for mid-European bodice, showing coloured "tunic-top" and white under-blouse effect: —

 Fig.16

When the two fabrics are joined together, cut away upper material showing the white cotton at the neck.

 Fig.17

Add lace, or felt or braids, or all three as desired. Always put braid over raw edges of top fabric, covering edges and securing the fabrics.

Join shoulders.
Add neck decorations, frills, or collar, as desired, on outside. (Facing on inside)

Fig.18

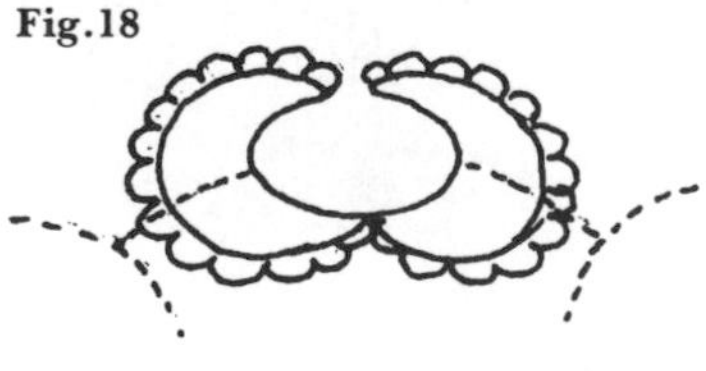

Fig.19

Fig.20

Fig.21

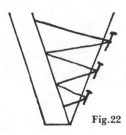

Fig.22

"Lacing" on corsage Pin
& tack corners, under
braid. Machine down
braid, over lacing, and all
will be secured.

Fig.23

Fig.24

Fig.25

C14th circa 1368

Prolong bodice to crutch
level and cut female neck-
line as low horizontally as
possible.

Support neckline by (a)
boning, as in tutu, or (b)
by narrow pink elastic over
shoulders.

C15th circa 1447

Cut away at neckline. Add fur trimming
after bodice is joined.
Base of bodice is well above natural
waistline.

Male bodice   add folds of
drapery after bodice is sewn
up.

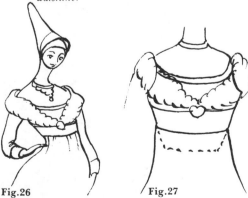

Fig.26

Fig.27

Fig.28

14

Fig.29

Fig.30

C16th Renaissance

Cover yoke with nylon chiffon. Cut a little wide so that it can be gathered into neckband and corsage.

Sew pearls on so that they do not flop about.

Fig.31

Male costume has slightly dropped waistline, extended to point at centre front.

Fig.32

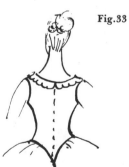

Fig.33

C18th

Pointed prolongation of bodice at front and back.

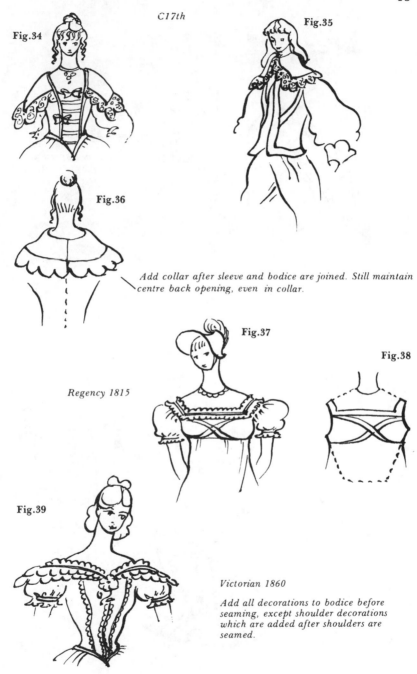

C17th

Fig.34

Fig.35

Fig.36

Add collar after sleeve and bodice are joined. Still maintain centre back opening, even in collar.

Fig.37

Fig.38

Regency 1815

Fig.39

Victorian 1860

Add all decorations to bodice before seaming, except shoulder decorations which are added after shoulders are seamed.

Fig.40

Edwardian, circa 1903

*"Pouched" appearance of bodice front.
Cut a little too long and tuck loosely into
tightly-fitting waistband at dropped waist
level.*

National Costume Bodices

Fig.41

Portuguese

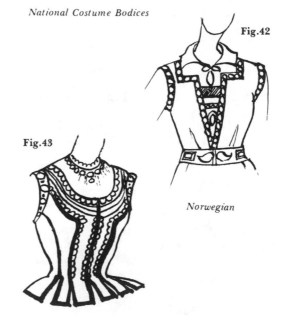

Fig.42

Fig.43

Norwegian

Polish

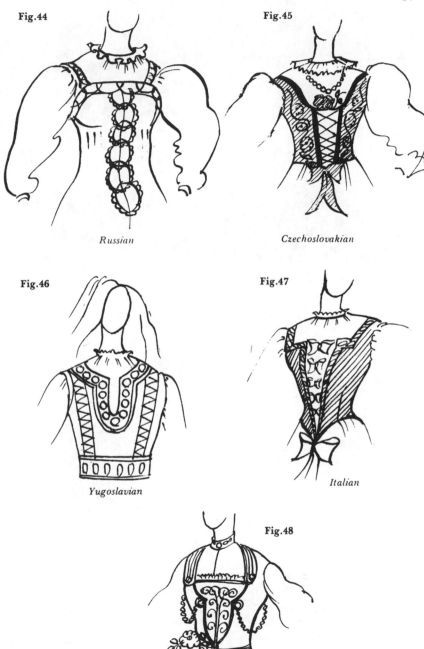

Fig.44 Russian

Fig.45 Czechoslovakian

Fig.46 Yugoslavian

Fig.47 Italian

Fig.48 Swiss

Plate 3.   Italian National Costume

Fig.49

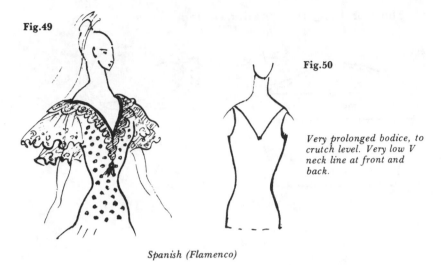

Spanish (Flamenco)

Fig.50

Very prolonged bodice, to crutch level. Very low V neck line at front and back.

SLEEVES, PANTALOONS

There is one important point in the construction of sleeves, and their insertion, for dancing costumes. So that the arms can be fully raised in dancing, armholes must be kept very high under the arm-pit, and very little "head" to the sleeve must be allowed.

A. Short or Long narrow sleeve

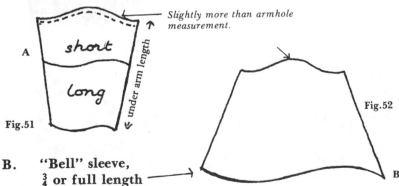

Slightly more than armhole measurement.

A

short

long

under arm length

Fig.51

Fig.52

B

B. **"Bell" sleeve, ¾ or full length**

C. Short or Long full "national" type sleeve

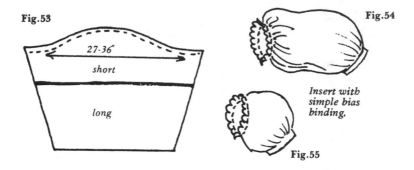

Fig.53

27-36"

short

long

Fig.54

Insert with
simple bias
binding.

Fig.55

D. Decorations, lace at cuff etc.
are added before sleeve seam is joined.

Fig.56

Join lace, flat, on to the lower edge.
Cover raw edges with a band of eyelet broderie Anglaise, thread with
elastic, black, or white dyed to match
dress.

If any other decoration down sleeve
is required, add this before joining up
sleeve, e.g. Fig.57.

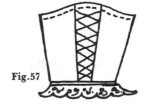

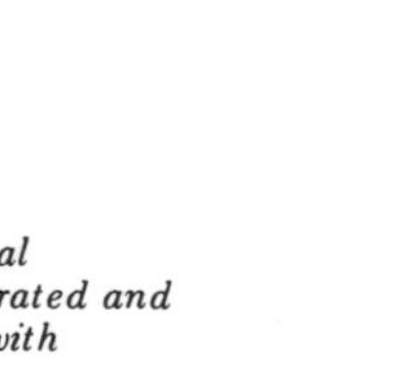

Fig.57

Fig.58

N.B. Pantaloons and National
Drawers. Lower edge is decorated and
drawn up in the same way, with
broiderie Anglaise, etc.

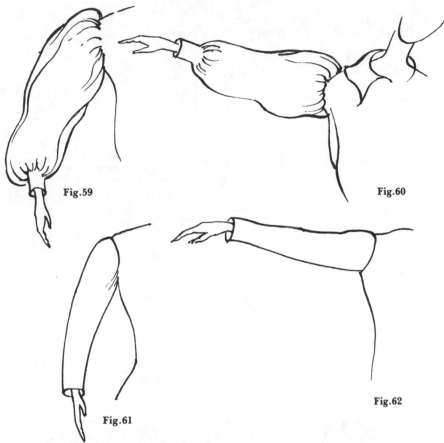

Fig.59

Fig.60

Fig.61

Fig.62

Sleeves for men's costumes correspond to female ones, with emphasis on the importance of free movement at the armpit — i.e. armhole of the garment is cut very high, very little "head" to sleeves being allowed.

Most classical and national (male) sleeves are simple shirt sleeves cut a little wider than normally, and always of a soft and flowing fabric. (Figs.59, 60).

Even jacket sleeves must have the same construction at the head. Although a few folds will appear at the armpits when the dancer stands in 1st position, these disappear immediately with any arm movement. (Figs.61, 62).

Sleeves for modern dance are usually simple shirt sleeves based on these classical examples.

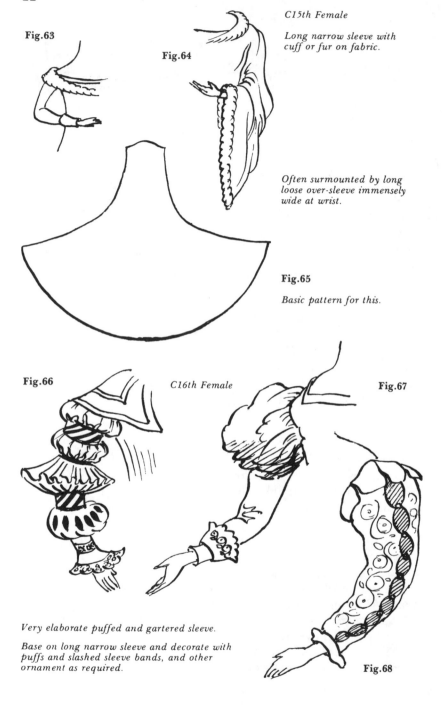

Fig.63

Fig.64

C15th Female

Long narrow sleeve with cuff or fur on fabric.

Often surmounted by long loose over-sleeve immensely wide at wrist.

Fig.65

Basic pattern for this.

Fig.66

C16th Female

Fig.67

Fig.68

Very elaborate puffed and gartered sleeve.

Base on long narrow sleeve and decorate with puffs and slashed sleeve bands, and other ornament as required.

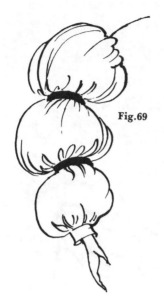

C16th Male costume sleeves

Gartered sleeves.

Cut sleeve very full in stiffish fabric such as poult or good taffeta. "Tie" in, where required, with bands of braid or ribbon.

Extra "bouffant" appearance may be given by stuffing sleeve top with crumpled balls of nylon net.

Fig.69

Tudor type "slashed" sleeve.

Make simple straight sleeve (Fig.71) and very full "puff" sleeve (Fig.72) and superimpose puff over straight sleeve. Cut "slashes", with pinking shears, in puff sleeves before seaming up (Fig.73) and stuff space between two layers tightly with coloured nylon net so that it almost protrudes through openings.

Insert both sleeves together into armhole as usual.

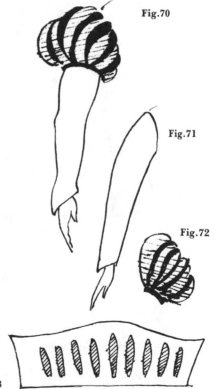

Fig.70

Fig.71

Fig.72

Fig.73

Fig.74

C16th Man's cloak sleeve

Very wide national sleeve with laced cuff.

C17th Stuart type

Long narrow "slashes" made by ribbon added to surface. Male.

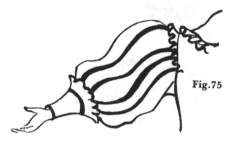

Fig.75

C17th

Ornate slashed sleeve with epaulette and laced cuff. Male.

Fig.76

C17th Female costume sleeve

Slashed puff at lower sleeve with wide open cuff.

Fig.77

C17th Male Costume sleeves

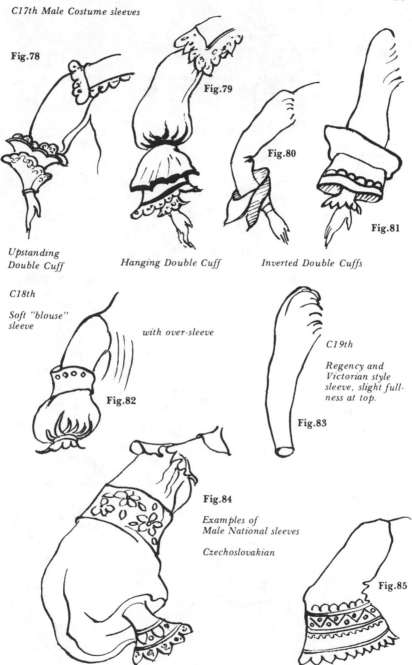

Fig.78

Fig.79

Fig.80

Fig.81

*Upstanding
Double Cuff*

Hanging Double Cuff

Inverted Double Cuffs

C18th

*Soft "blouse"
sleeve*

with over-sleeve

Fig.82

C19th

*Regency and
Victorian style
sleeve, slight full-
ness at top.*

Fig.83

Fig.84

*Examples of
Male National sleeves*

Czechoslovakian

Fig.85

Fig.86

Swiss — short jacket sleeve with white national sleeve beneath.

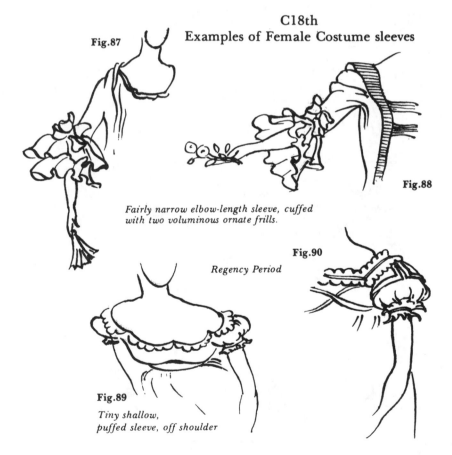

C18th
Examples of Female Costume sleeves

Fig.87

Fairly narrow elbow-length sleeve, cuffed with two voluminous ornate frills.

Fig.88

Fig.90

Regency Period

Fig.89

Tiny shallow, puffed sleeve, off shoulder

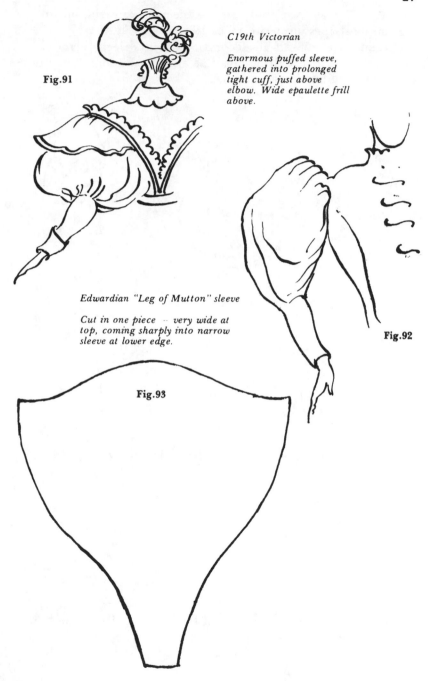

Fig.91

C19th Victorian

Enormous puffed sleeve, gathered into prolonged tight cuff, just above elbow. Wide epaulette frill above.

Edwardian "Leg of Mutton" sleeve

Cut in one piece — very wide at top, coming sharply into narrow sleeve at lower edge.

Fig.92

Fig.93

Most Female National costume sleeves are variations of the simple shapes given on pages 19 and 20 (Figs.51-57).

Remember to add all decorations *before* sleeve seam is joined, when fabric can be laid flat and "embroidery" can be stuck, or appliqued, on to sleeve.

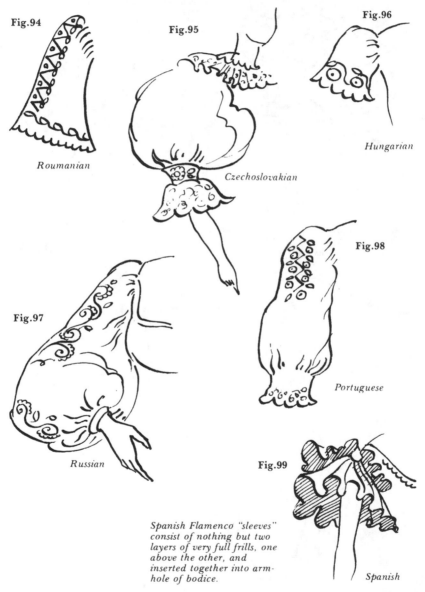

Fig.94

Roumanian

Fig.95

Czechoslovakian

Fig.96

Hungarian

Fig.97

Russian

Fig.98

Portuguese

Fig.99

Spanish Flamenco "sleeves" consist of nothing but two layers of very full frills, one above the other, and inserted together into arm-hole of bodice.

Spanish

Plate 4.   Swedish National Costume

SKIRT

Simple gathered skirt.

Make a fitting belt of white petersham 1½″ wide, closed with two firm hooks and eyes.

Fig.100

Cut 3 or 4 widths, according to requirements, of the skirt-length needed, and join them, selvedge to selvedge.

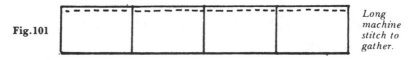

Fig.101 — *Long machine stitch to gather.*

Add decorations, and adjust hem before pulling up gathers and joining back seam.

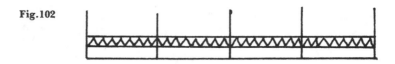

Fig.102

Draw up top gathers and arrange on to the petersham band.

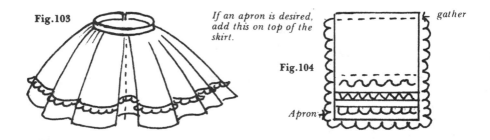

Fig.103

If an apron is desired, add this on top of the skirt.

Fig.104

gather

Apron

Assembly of Bodice and Skirt.
Leave gathered, raw edges. If there is no sash, arrange the base of the bodice, turned under once, over the raw edges of skirt, and hem or stitch on to the petersham band. Fig.106.

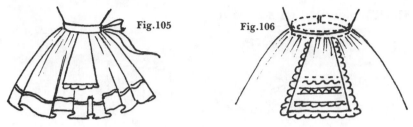

Fig.105   Fig.106

If there is a sash, the bodice need not be turned under, as raw edges of both bodice and skirt are covered by the sash.

Ukranian National Costume

SKIRT mounted on a Basque

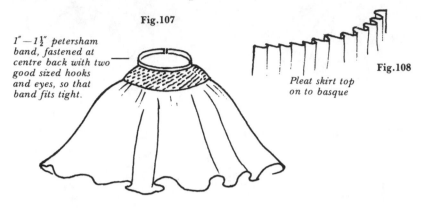

Fig.107

1" — 1½" petersham band, fastened at centre back with two good sized hooks and eyes, so that band fits tight.

Fig.108

Pleat skirt top on to basque

Cut **Basque** shape in strong cotton. (The strong sides from old sheets are splendid).

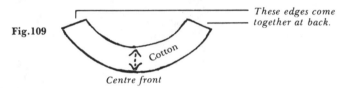

Fig.109

These edges come together at back.

Cotton

Centre front

Pin inner edge on to petersham band and fit.

Fig.110

Cotton

Then remove from band, marking pin positions with pencil.

On unmarked side, lay the cotton basque on to the desired fabric, pin the two fabrics together, and using the cotton as a pattern cut out the top fabric.
Using the two fabrics from now onwards as one, pin them on to the petersham band again, and stitch.

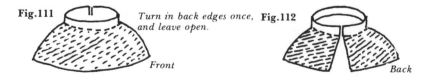

Fig.111

Turn in back edges once, and leave open.

Fig.112

Front

Back

Plate 5.   Czechoslovakian National Costume for the "Ribbon Dance"

Cut the required number of widths of desired length, and join selvedges. The length should allow $\frac{1}{2}''$ at the top for joining on to the basque (see pleating note Fig.108) and 1″ for hem — or more if desired.

Before joining on to basque, make hem and add any decorative bands or frills etc. while skirt is still *laid out flat*.

Fig.113

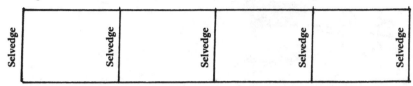

Next, *pleat* on to the outside of the lower edge of the basque, as pleats lie more neatly than gathers. Cover join with decorative braid or bias binding.

Finally join the back seam, leaving 6″ open, and add press-studs down the back opening.

CIRCULAR SKIRT

Cut length of 1″ wide petersham band to fit waist tightly.
Fasten with two firm hooks and eyes.

Fig.115

Fig.114

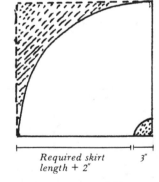

Required skirt length + 2″   *3″*

If the skirt is very small or the material very wide, it can be made in one piece, seamless.
(Make a newspaper pattern first.)

Cut a square of paper, each side being the required skirt length plus 5″. With a 2′ rule, mark off dots, equidistant from one corner. Join dots, and cut away corner, also a small segment of about 3″ radius at corner. Fold material twice and place pattern on the corner (four thicknesses after folding) and cut out. The wider the material, the longer the possible skirt length.

If a longer skirt is needed, cut in two sections, seaming at centre front and back up to top 6″ (for opening).

Fig.116

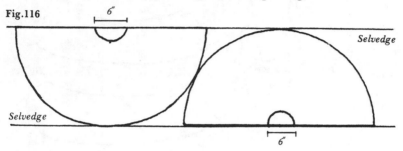

Cut small waist circle, smaller than is needed as it can easily be enlarged, but cannot be reduced neatly. Add extra length to allow for this adjustment, 2″ − 3″ and use cut off strips from lower edge for use as bias facing or binding.

After attaching to petersham at waist, and before adjusting hem line, allow to "hang" for several days, so that material can "drop". Even up the hem and face. Leave the back seam open for upper 8″. Sides will be selvedges, so there is no need to hem them.

Decorations are more easily added before 2 sections are seamed together, keeping pieces laid out flat.

Fig.117   Fig.118

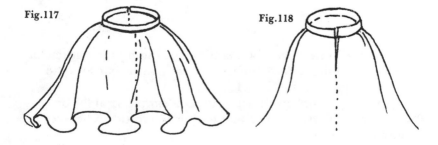

Classical "Drape" type skirts should merely give an idea of a true skirt, the line being maintained by the underlying leotard, and should be made of very soft fabric such as chiffon, georgette or nylon chiffon.

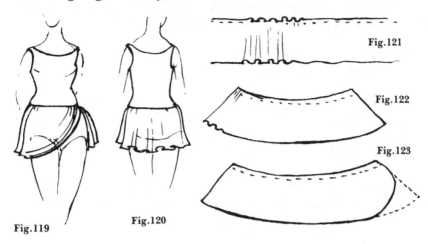

Fig.121

Fig.122

Fig.123

Fig.119

Fig.120

Either cut straight and gather a little at the top (Fig.119, 120, 121), or make a slight curve (Fig.122) to give a more flared effect. The flared skirt is best cut in two pieces, each cut a little wider than necessary, and drawn up to fit at hip level (Fig.124).

Fig.124

Fig.125

"Draped" effects can be made by arranging the gathers at one side, as desired. Sometimes a corner can be cut away to enhance a curve, as in Fig. 119, 123.

For "looped-up" overskirts, cut as a simple straight or slightly flared skirt. Cut full and gather up vertically where required (Fig.125).

EMPIRE LINE SKIRTS

Skirts attached at bust level such as were worn from about 1800-1830, and many national costumes, need special attention.

Although they are not joined to the petersham band as usual, at the waist, it is still best to make the cotton foundation with the waistband. Any petticoats required can then be joined to this band, and the "bust" bodice be firmly made on to it, as in other bodices.

As the base edge of the skirt must be a full circle in width, it is best to make a normal circular skirt as described in Figs.114, 115, 116, 117, 118. The radius of this circle being the entire length from bust to hem.

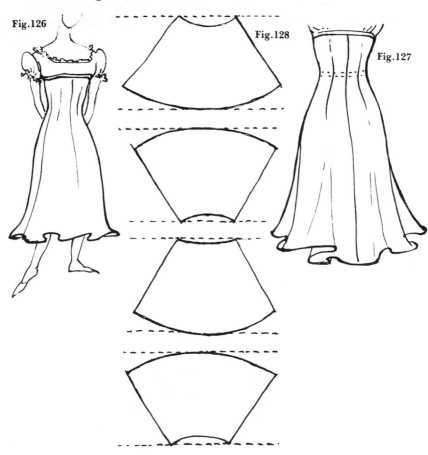

Fig.126

Fig.128

Fig.127

38

Unless the fabric is unusually wide, it will be necessary to cut it in four pieces (Fig.128).

Join centre front, back and side seams, and pin to leotard at bust level.

Carefully fit by darting to natural waistline level at the four seams, and also half-way between each of these — in eight places in all.

Allow darts to taper off to a fine point and disappear about ⅔ down the length of the skirt.

The centre back opening extends to hip level and must be carefully closed with hooks and eyes, making sure the finish is "edge-to-edge".

Sometimes slight gathering is required at the top, in which case the circular skirt is cut with a larger centre circle than actually required, the fullness being gathered in and adjusted to the leotard.

Assemble with bodice in the same way at bust level as at waist level.

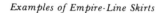

Examples of Empire-Line Skirts

Fig.129

Fig.130

Fig.131

Fig.132

Russian or Polish Court costumes have long "Empire Line" skirts flowing from the bustline (Fig.133).

National Russian (peasant) type skirts (Fig.134) should give the effect of a simple gathered length, attached at bust level. In fact they look much less "bulky" at the top if cut on a slight flare in four pieces.

There will be a join at centre front, easily hidden by decoration, one at each side and one at the centre back.

All decorations at lower edge are attached before skirt is joined to leotard at bust level.

Fig.134

Fig.133

Fig.135

¼ of skirt Cut 4

Length from bust to lower edge.

The Victorian voluminous skirt, or rather the illusion of it, is used by dancers in the form of the romantic tutu described in a later section.

The true Victorian crinoline skirt is not suitable as the wire cage would impede dance movements. However, the effect of this is given by banking up layer upon layer of nylon net petticoat, as described under "Skirt on a Basque" (Figs.107-113), and national or character petticoats (Figs.144, 145, 146).

Sometimes the bodice is prolonged to a point at centre front (Fig.137). However the skirt should be made as usual, and the bodice drawn down here, over the gathers, to form a point. Gather a little less at centre front just beneath the bodice point.

Fig.136

Fig.137

Every fabric for the foundation garment must be feather-light and never made of a heavy cotton as in fact they were at the time. The top skirt is simply a straight piece decorated and gathered at the top.

Fig.138

Fig.139

The late Victorian and Edwardian bustle was also supported by various forms of wire cage and padding, but this is unnecessary and unwise in the dance costume.

Sufficient lift at the back may be obtained by arranging as many of the gatherings as possible at the back, leaving the front of the skirt to fall almost ungathered, smooth and straight from the waist.

A small amount of light padding may be used at the back if the bustle effect is to be emphasised. However, the addition of a large bow or drape at the back gives a good illusion without restricting movement (Figs.138, 139, 140).

Fig.140

SKIRTS FOR SPANISH FLAMENCO DANCERS OF SOUTHERN SPAIN

These are based on full circular skirts, sometimes with added quarter circle segment to give even more width.

The skirts are decorated with at least three very full flounces which are attached to the circular base in exactly the same way as the frills for the "National Petticoat" (Figs.144-146). The top of the uppermost flounce is attached at the dropped waistline at hip level and the join covered by bringing the lengthened bodice down to meet it. The join is covered with braid, fringing or bobble-fringe.

Each flounce should cut wide enough to encircle the skirt twice at the level required. Decorate lower edge of flounces with lace, fringe or bobble-braid, as desired, before gathering them up to arrange on the skirt.

Sometimes a "train" effect is desired at the back (Fig.141), in which case an extra flounce may be added beneath the others, and all the flounces can be widened at the back. An even more pronounced train can be made by adding an extremely wide, very full flounce vertically from hip to floor. This can be gathered down the centre of the strip to give a "doubled" effect (Fig.143).

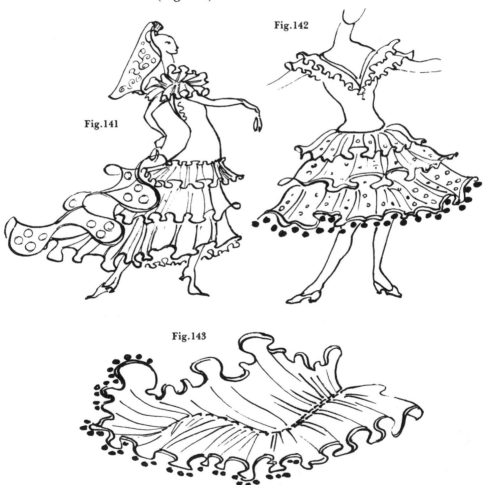

Fig.141

Fig.142

Fig.143

Plate 6. Spanish (Jota) National Costume

PETTICOAT for National and Character Costumes

Cut out skirt in white cotton or nylon material as for a circular skirt. Join seams and allow to "hang" for several days. Do not attach to petersham band (except with pins for fitting) until all frills and laces are added.

Attach lace to lower edge (when "hang drop" has been adjusted). Lay out flat and prepare for frills.

Using a ruler, as for circular skirt, mark out 3 concentric circles, in pencil, on right side, approx. $\frac{1}{4}$, $\frac{1}{2}$ and $\frac{3}{4}$ up length of skirt.

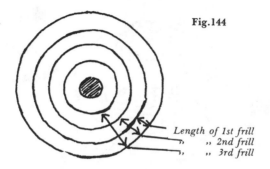

Fig.144

Length of 1st frill
„ „ 2nd frill
„ „ 3rd frill

Using white nylon net, cut three long strips across width of material (54″ wide) each of 4 widths (4 x 54″) and arrange lengths so that all 3 just reach lower edge of the circular skirt. (See fig.144.)

Join the 4 widths of each frill, and if possible, add lace at lower edge of each.

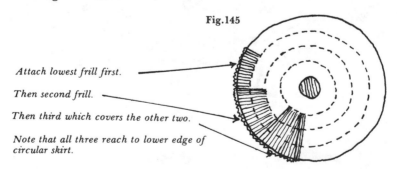

Fig.145

Attach lowest frill first.

Then second frill.

Then third which covers the other two.

Note that all three reach to lower edge of circular skirt.

If possible add lace or Broderie Anglaise to edge of circular skirt, also to as many of the frills as can be afforded.

This petticoat can *either* be incorporated under the top skirt of any costume, *or* used as an entirely separate garment.

Fig.146

Can Can Costume

APRONS

Aprons are used extensively in dance costume and are attractive adornments adding character, or nationality, to a skirt. They may be basically functional in appearance, as in the Victorian pinafore, or purely decorative, as those used on the "Coppelia" skirts. They add valuable folk design information to national costumes of which they form a very important part.

Fig.147

Care must be taken that they are lightly but firmly attached to the skirt, near the lower edge, otherwise they will flip up and twist over, and all decorative effect will be lost, leaving a "muddled" effect.

Attach to top layer(s) of skirt here

The Victorian Apron

Treat this as a "decorated bodice" and "aproned skirt" (Figs.105 and 106). Assemble both to the petersham, covering raw edges with the apron band, sewn down at both edges.

Add made bow at back (Figs.196-199). All edges are decorated with Broderie Anglais and eyelet braid threaded with black ribband.

Fig.148

The Edwardian or late Victorian "Pinny"

This is sometimes used as an overdress, of a contrasting fabric, or as a white "Pinny" for domesticity. It is always decorated with Broderie Anglais and eyelet braid.

Fig.149

Ideally, it should be cut in one piece, but an invisible join at waist level is permissible, provided that the darting and fit are good.

Finish at the back with bow and shoulder bands, as with Victorian apron (Fig.148).

Men's Aprons

Fig.150
*Farmer, Cobbler, Gardener,
etc.*

Fig.151

Butcher, Tradesman etc.

National Costume

Fig.153

Fig.152

Czechoslovakian

Swedish

Aprons for National Costumes (female)

Fig.154

Small vertical pleats, sewn in for 1½"—2" and allowed to fall free below this level

Apron sash crosses back, and is finished with made bow in front. (Sash completely stitched down all round — neat invisible join for back opening.)

Dutch

Fig.155

Very light and lacy

Hungarian

The variation in National Costume aprons is enormous, and the number of shapes, sizes and colours, not even including the decorations, is limitless.

Shape, and the proportion in size to the skirt, is as important as the designs upon them, and this must be considered first before any decoration is added.

The examples shown here are only a sample of the vast number to be found on national costumes, but may give some idea of the types and variations.

As with skirts, all decorations are added *before* the apron is drawn up at the top and attached. When both skirt and apron are ready and fully decorated, stitch them on to the petersham band, firstly the skirt and then the apron at centre front (or where desired). Cover raw edges with bodice or apron sash.

52

Most alpine national aprons, like the skirts, are light and lacy and much gathered to aid the "bouffant" effect, very romantic.

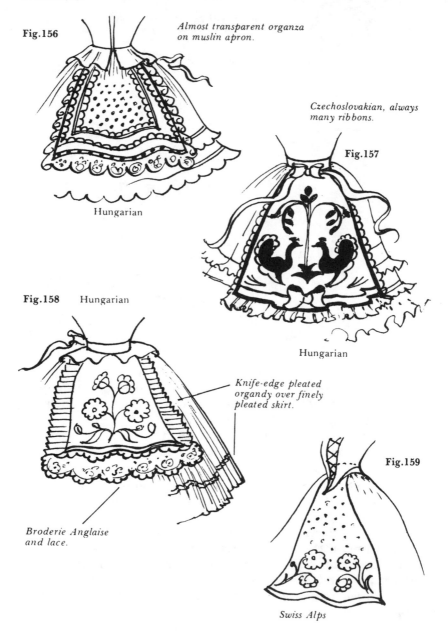

Fig.156

Almost transparent organza on muslin apron.

Hungarian

Czechoslovakian, always many ribbons.

Fig.157

Hungarian

Fig.158   Hungarian

Knife-edge pleated organdy over finely pleated skirt.

Broderie Anglaise and lace.

Fig.159

Swiss Alps

Fig.160

German

Swiss

Fig.161

The Swiss and French aprons (Figs.161 and 162), and many other national aprons, are not true aprons but part overskirts, covering the front only.

Wherever the bodice is prolonged and/or comes to a point below the national waistline, the apron (with the skirt) is attached to the petersham band, as usual. The bodice is then drawn down and lightly hemmed to apron and top layers of the skirt and petticoats, as well as being securely through-stitched (by hand) on to the petersham band at waistline.

French (Limousin)

Spanish

Fig.162

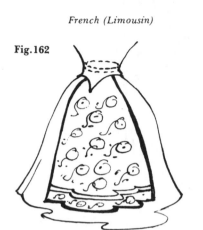

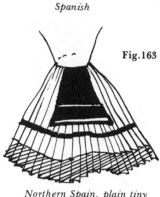

Fig.163

Northern Spain, plain tiny and black, slightly gathered at top.

Fig.164

Salamanca long black apron, richly embroidered and showing moorish influence.

Fig.165

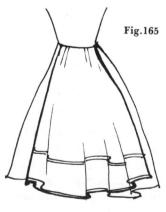

Central and Western Spain, Extramaduras long, plain and black, with touch of red braid.

Spanish

Fig.166

Fig.167

Top of apron is shaped like part of a "basque" and lower part is gathered on to lower edge of this.

Fig.168

Polish

Fig.169

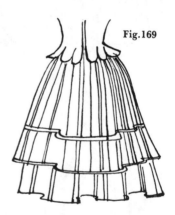

The apron often completely encircles the Polish skirt and becomes an overskirt.

Fig.170

Aprons from the Balkans are heavy and straight, usually being made of thick folk-woven wool. They are decorated with interwoven designs of traditional geometric patterns suitable for the weaver's craft.

Fig.171

Fig.172

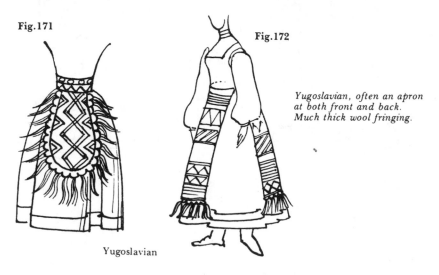

Yugoslavian, often an apron at both front and back. Much thick wool fringing.

Yugoslavian

Fig.173

Fig.174

Fig.175

Greek (not ancient)

Materials a little finer than Yugoslavian but still of finely woven wool. Decoration a little more delicate. Much wool fringe and gold thread embroidery, with red, black and cream weaving.

Plate 7.   Hungarian National Costume

Plate 8.   Czechoslovakian National Costume for a child

DECORATIONS

These should be simple and bold, of good clear design, emphasizing essential characteristics, remembering that fine detail is lost when seen from an auditorium.

Elaborate designs must be simplified, and the use of felt and appliqued fabrics, to assimilate embroidery, is much to be recommended.

DECORATION OF THE MIDDLE AGES COSTUMES

Fur

Fur was used a great deal throughout this period as trimmings on cloaks, for collars and cuffs and decorative borders, both on male and female costumes.

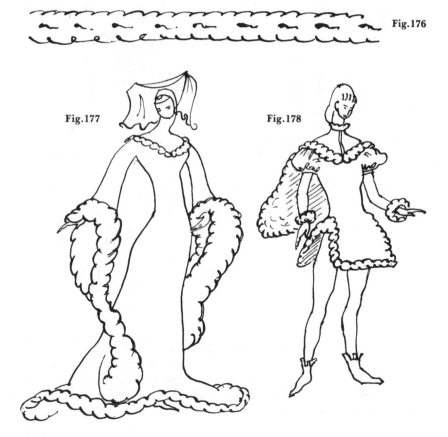

Fig.176

Fig.177   Fig.178

Nylon or synthetic fur fabric is cheaply and easily obtained today and this is best bought by the yard and cut into strips of the required width with pinking shears. This does not fray and can be stitched or stuck on (with UHU) where required.

Fig.179

Fig.180

"Ermine" trimmings are made by using strips of white fur fabric or nylon wadding, also bought by the yard and cut into strips in the same way. When it is attached to the garment, black marks are made as "tails", where desired, with a wide felt-tipped marker pen (Fig.176).

"Gold" and "silver" decorations are best made with gold and silver lurex fabric, bought by the yard and cut into strips, or the required shape, with pinking shears. Machine into position on garment at either edge, and cover stitching with narrow decorative braid (Fig.181).

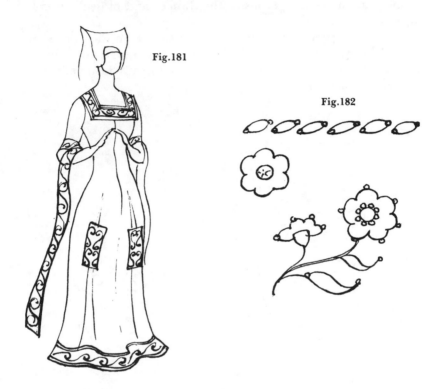

Fig.181

Fig.182

If there is to be design or jewellery *on* the lurex, it is best to mount the gold or silver shape on to vilene and add jewellery or other decorations at this stage before attaching to garment, as described above.

Such designs can be made with "Russia" braid in black or some contrasting colour, while most lurex fabrics will take a marker pen design simply drawn on. This must be tried out first, however, to make sure the ink does not run (Fig.181).

Gold leaves and flowers can be of lurex material cut out with pinking shears. A few "pearls" or glass "jewellery" sewn over these will secure both lurex and brilliant to the underlying fabric and give a rich effect.

62

Jewellery

All necklaces, pendants, bracelets, head-dress decorations, etc., must be firmly attached to underlying garment, in fact becoming extra adornments to the bodice, cuff, head-dress, etc., rather than separate "jewellery". This prevents them from flapping about — dangerous to the dancer and most distracting to the audience.

The only permissable necklace appearing on the bare skin is the "choker", immovable, fitting the neck, usually of velvet with jewel decorations upon it. It must be firmly fastened at the back with hooks and eyes.

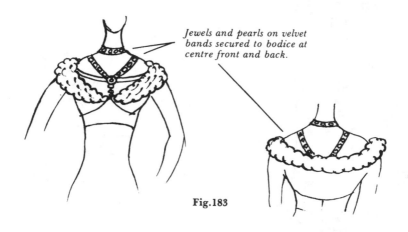

Jewels and pearls on velvet bands secured to bodice at centre front and back.

Fig. 183

Excellent imitation pearls and glass jewellery — emeralds, rubies, sapphires, topaz, crystal, rose quartz, etc., — can be obtained at theatrical suppliers, very cheaply, and beautiful and rich effects can be made by the tasteful use of these. With the exception of some national costume decorations, restriction of colour choice of these is desirable. For instance, gold, silver and pearl "jewels" look extremely well together, as do crystal, sapphire and aquamarine, or silver and rose glass with pearls. Emerald goes with gold. However, too many colours simply cancel themselves out and become vulgar.

Gold and silver "chain", often used as girdles on men's costumes, can also be bought at theatrical stores. They must be carefully attached in many places to ensure that they do not flap about with the movement.

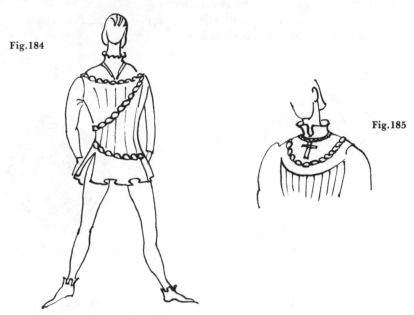

Fig.184

Fig.185

Tudor and Stuart Period

The use of felt in combination with imitation jewels is most effective. In elaborate Tudor period costumes, for instance, whole bodice fronts may be covered with decorative felt shapes and made brilliant with glass jewels, pearls, gold and silver lurex, sequins, etc.

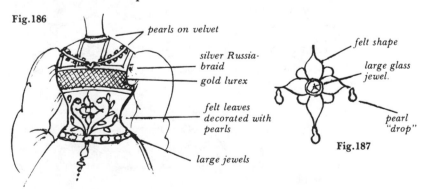

Fig.186

pearls on velvet

silver Russia-braid

gold lurex

felt leaves decorated with pearls

large jewels

felt shape

large glass jewel.

pearl "drop"

Fig.187

Very small decorations, such as tiny jewels, are not worth using as they are insignificant. All ornament must be simple, clear and bold if it is to be "read" by the audience.

A useful way to show gold chain is to cut felt leaves and attach each to garments in chain order.

Gold lurex is even more effective but each leaf must be mounted on vilene before attaching.

Fig.188

Fig.189

C18th and C19th Ornaments

The Cameo brooch can be made very effectively from felt and gold Russia braid.

First cut the basic oval shape in peach coloured felt and mount this on vilene. Cut the simple silhouette shape in white or cream and stick this on with UHU. Add gold Russia braid — plain or crossed over in places, round the edge (Fig.189). Attach to dress where desired.

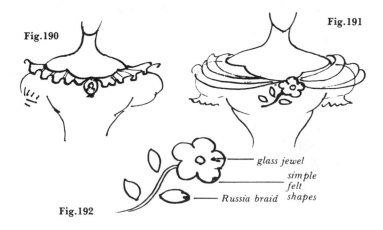

Fig.190

Fig.191

glass jewel

simple felt shapes

Russia braid

Fig.192

Although bought artificial flowers are usually used for corsage ornaments, felt ones are made more cheaply and are very decorative.

Draped "scallops" are made from nylon organza or stiff nylon chiffon.

On a straight length of required width, gather up vertical lines at regular intervals and secure.

Tack lightly on to garment at gathered points.

Avoid using this decoration at extreme base of skirt as it may catch the foot and cause a mishap.

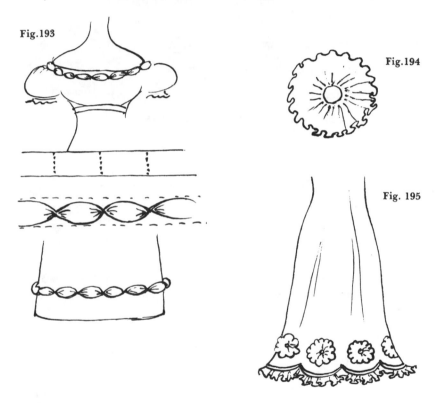

Fig.193

Fig.194

Fig. 195

Flat "flowers" can be made by gathering up strips of ribband or poult along one edge and securing them to the garment with a jewel at the centre. The outer edge should also be tacked down in a few places to avoid "flopping".

Complement this decoration with gathered ribband "ruching" or a frill (Figs.194, 195).

Bows. Do not rely on tying these at the time of wearing. They will not look "natural" or tidy. Always sew them firmly beforehand, and if necessary use a snapper just behind knot of bow, if in a position to require un-doing to put on.

Simple way of making bows.

The bow-fabric should always be stiffened with nylon-net. If fabric is used, and not ribbon, this must be cut into strips with pinking shears.

Fabric backed with nylon net, and cut into strips.

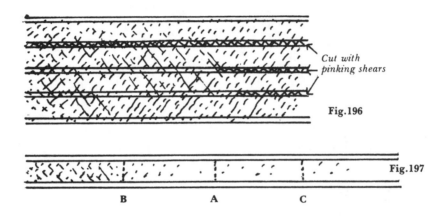

Cut with pinking shears

Fig.196

Fig.197

B   A   C

Gather nylon-net backed fabric at B, A and C, and place B and C behind A, and stitch all together firmly.

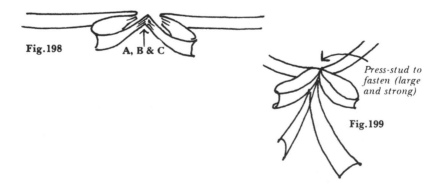

Fig.198   A, B & C

Press-stud to fasten (large and strong)

Fig.199

Victorian Ornament

Lace, braids and all kinds of elaborate decoration were used at this time, mostly made laboriously by hand. Effective ways of showing this on costume, however, need not be in the least tedious, the less so the better in fact as simplified detail enhances the illusion.

One most effective decorative braid is the material "scallop strip". This could hardly be easier to make and can be used simply by itself, or as a cover over the join of a flounce to a skirt, for example. This is particularly useful in national costumes.

Stitch to garment here   Fig.200

Make a paper pattern of about six scallops of the desired width, and repeat it to make a long strip — a yard or so if it is for a skirt. Pin the pattern (repeatedly) on the fabric and cut out the strip with pinking shears (unless felt is being used in which case ordinary scissors are better), and continue until full required length is cut.

Attach to garment with single line of machine stitching a little within the straight edge (Fig.200).

Cover this edge and stitching with narrow braid, bias strip, seam binding or ribband.

The scallops may themselves be covering the join of frill to skirt as in Fig.202. This is an easy and delightful decoration and can be used in many period costumes, as well as on many national and "character" ones.

Fig.201

Fig.202

Decorations for "National" and "Character" skirts are best made on a separate strip of fabric. Nylon net, of the skirt colour, or white, is the best material for this. When this strip is fully decorated it is added to the skirt, before the back seam of this is sewn up and before the top gathers (or pleats) are drawn up. It should be tacked on lightly, and then seamed by a band of braid or other narrow decoration which is machined through this, the strip, and the skirt.

The decoration is then removable, and both the skirt and the "embroidery" can be used again and independently for another costume. This also applies to decorations on sleeves and bodices.

Floral shapes etc. can be cut out of felt, or from any fabric which does not "fray", and this must be cut with pinking shears.

Fabrics can be tacked on, or stuck on with "UHU".

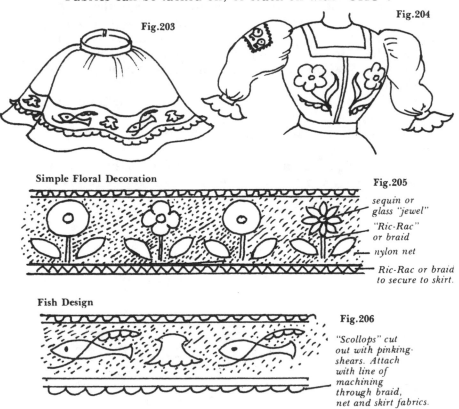

Fig.203

Fig.204

Simple Floral Decoration

Fig.205

sequin or glass "jewel"

"Ric-Rac" or braid

nylon net

Ric-Rac or braid to secure to skirt.

Fish Design

Fig.206

"Scollops" cut out with pinking-shears. Attach with line of machining through braid, net and skirt fabrics.

Peacock Design   Fig.207

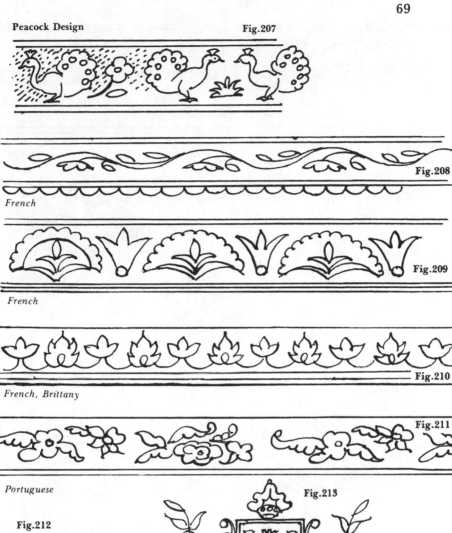

Fig.208

French

Fig.209

French

Fig.210

French, Brittany

Fig.211

Portuguese

Fig.212

*Portuguese repeated
panels in red, black
and cream*

Fig.213

*Skirt decoration in
silver on dark blue
or black.*

Portuguese

Fig.214

Italian

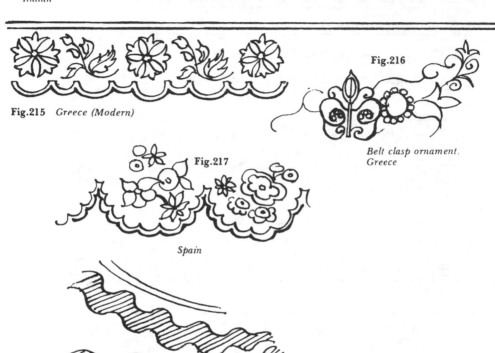

Fig.216

Fig.215 *Greece (Modern)*

Belt clasp ornament.
Greece

Fig.217

Spain

Fig.218

Shawl decoration, Extramaduras, Spain
appears like very wide "ric-rac" braid.
Cut in red felt and stick on to black
shawls etc.

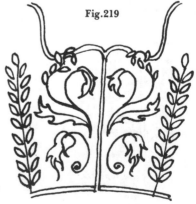

Fig.219

Navarre, Spain, feathery corsage
decoration in gold and silver on red or
black.

Fig.220

*Yugoslavian. Woven
decorative pattern.*

Fig.221

Yugoslav skirt decoration

Decoration of Male Dancers' Costumes

Special care should be taken over these costumes. The decorations should emphasise boldness and clarity and avoid "prettiness" so that the contrast between the male and female costumes is underlined.

Although really a question for the designer, the costume-maker should look for masculinity in detail rather than charm, strength rather than delicacy.

Plate 9.   Italian Tarantella, 1830 National Costume

HEAD-DRESSES

There is no doubt that a head-dress can make or mar an entire costume.

The impact of character, period or nationality should be immediately felt the moment the dancer appears, and nothing affects this more directly than the correct head-dress.

Accuracy of fit and simplicity of design are of great importance, as is also the necessity of secure fastening to the head, so that it does not become dislodged with dancing.

Whenever possible, avoid covering any part of the neck. Drapery here spoils the vital continuity of the line and interrupts the flow of the movement. Any veils absolutely necessary, for instance, in some mediaeval costume should be made of very soft flowing fabric, almost transparent, such as nylon chiffon so that as much of the neckline as possible can at least be guessed at if not actually seen.

Every effort should be made to avoid head-dresses which hide the face such as wide-brimmed hats and bonnets, otherwise the facial expressions will be lost. Arrange such brims well back on the head so that they do not cast a shadow over the face.

Buckram and milliner's wire are the most useful materials for making head-dresses. They are easy to handle, and are extremely effective. Actual head fittings can be made if a wooden "block" is available, over which wet buckram is stretched and moulded into the required shape. When dry, the buckram retains the shape moulded on the block.

An alternative method is to cut out the approximate shapes required in newspaper, using sellotape to join them together, obtaining the correct "shape and fit" by "trial and error". The pieces are then used as a pattern, when corrected, to cut out the shapes in buckram.

Edge each piece of Buckram with milliner's wire, by oversewing, and then join them together by stitching over both milliner's wires at rims.

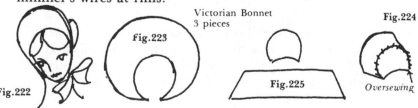

Fig.222

Fig.223

Victorian Bonnet
3 pieces

Fig.224

Fig.225

Oversewing

If any of the pieces are to be decorated, this is best done before they are joined together. If they are to be covered, this should also be done first, before joining and decorating, but after wiring.

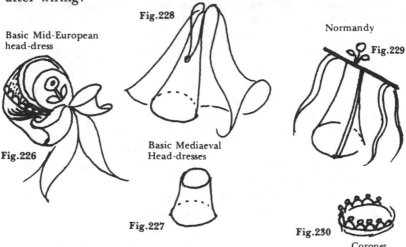

Basic Mid-European head-dress

Fig.226

Fig.228

Basic Mediaeval Head-dresses

Fig.227

Normandy

Fig.229

Fig.230

Coronet

Fixing of head-dresses to the top of head.

This is most important, as the movement loosens all but the firmest fastenings. Base all "on top of head" head-dresses on a wire frame, slightly curved to fit the top of the head, and filled in with veiling or doubled nylon net. (Fig.231).

milliner's wire

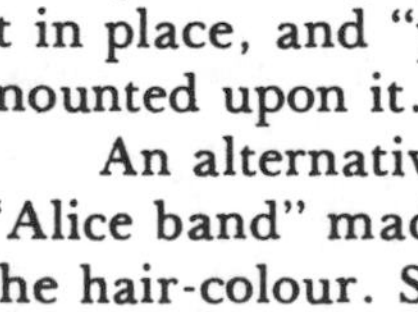

Fig.231

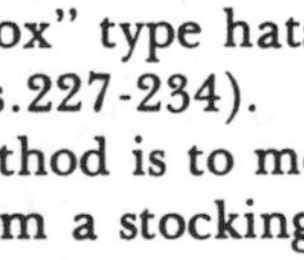

Fig.232

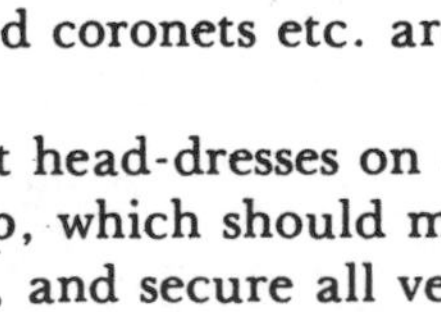

Fig.233

Hair-pins and grips are put through both net and hair to keep it in place, and "pill-box" type hats and coronets etc. are mounted upon it. (Figs.227-234).

An alternative method is to mount head-dresses on an "Alice band" made from a stocking-top, which should match the hair-colour. Sew head-dress to this, and secure all very firmly with grips and hair-pins. This is ideal for ballet coronets, etc. (Fig.235).

Fig.234

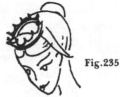

Fig.235

When head-dresses, such as bonnets are tied under the chin, do not rely on this to keep it in place. Many grips and pins are also necessary, and the net frame is also needed.

These examples of head-dresses can all be made quite simply if the above instructions are applied.

Fig.236   *Middle Ages*

Gold lurex over buckram. Glass jewels. Heavy net veiling, if possible in gold, over own or padded extra false hair.

Fig.237

Buckram brim and crown are covered with fur fabric before joining.

Fig.238

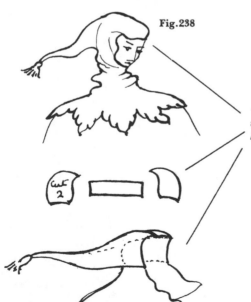

"Balaclava" helmet pattern with extensions to all three pieces at back edges.

Fig.239

Soft felt cap. Can be made from flower pot shape felt without wiring.

The "Steeple" Middle Ages head-dress with very long veil (often as long as the dress) is only used for quiet slow dances as it is too difficult to manoeuvre, especially in group work. It must be extremely securely fastened to the head with a wire frame (Fig.231).

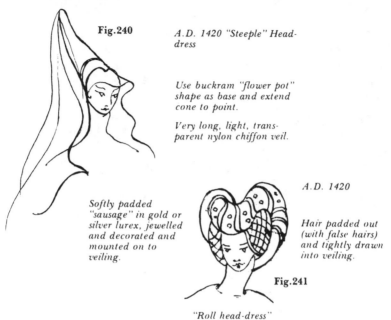

Fig.240

A.D. 1420 "Steeple" Head-dress

Use buckram "flower pot" shape as base and extend cone to point.

Very long, light, transparent nylon chiffon veil.

A.D. 1420

Softly padded "sausage" in gold or silver lurex, jewelled and decorated and mounted on to veiling.

Hair padded out (with false hairs) and tightly drawn into veiling.

Fig.241

"Roll head-dress"

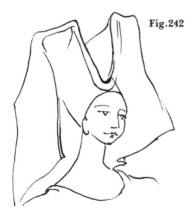

Fig.242

"Wing" head-dress A.D. 1462

Fig.243

Wire support for winged head-dress.

Fig.244

Elizabethan

A.D. 1530

Simple buck-ram crescent shape lavishly decorated

A.D. 1560

Fig.245

Fig.246

A.D. 1510

Man's wide "soft" hat made of felt, unwired

A.D. 1530

Fig.247

Fig.248

Baroque

A.D. 1665

Man's hat in felt, tall crown, wide brim

Fig.249

Man's "Tricorn" hat "pork pie" crown in felt with wide brim caught up and stitched to crown in 3 places

C18th

Tall hat with wired and up-bent brim. Ostrich feathers and bows

Regency Period

Fig.250

Victorian

Lace and ribbons

The "Snood" hair-net

Fig.251

*Bonnet with brim
set far back on head*

Fig.252

Edwardian

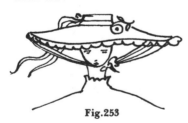

Fig.253

*Only use if character demands —
brim hides face*

Fig.254

National Head-dresses

Italian (Campania)

French (Burgundy)

Fig.255

Fig.256

Crisply gathered up nylon net drawn through buckram ring – one end opened out to "sit" on the head (and wire frame). Lace "ribbon" tails and bow.

Support firmly with wire frame and attach securely to top of head

Spanish Mantilla

Fig.257

Fig.258

Spanish comb and black lace Mantilla comb must have wire support round "bun" for extra firmness

Fig.259

Fix top to rollers (hair curlers)

Italian (Calabria) Man's tall hat in felt with veil-like sunshield at back in coarse cotton

Alternative method of securing flat Italian head-dresses

Danish

Fig.260

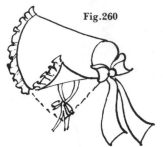

Cut in buckram and turn
up prolonged corners

Swiss

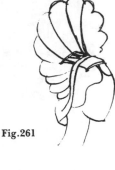

Fig.261

Arrange wire frame so that it lies from front to
back on head. Cut lace (black) shape first,
gathering slightly into band, and add "spokes"
of black milliners' wire from edge to band and
then bend back along frame

Fig.262

Enormous buckram brim, no crown but
top piled up with flowers.

Use large wire frame, decorating it and
making it part of the head-dress

Dutch

Fig.263

Gold "curls" of
wired gold Russia
braid

Crisply starched and wired
lace

Make wire frame (Fig.231)
in white, cover with lace
and use as feature of head-
dress

Dutch

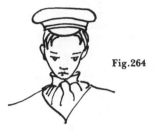

Fig.264

*Stiff buckram brim and
soft felt top*

Russian

Fig.265

*Place decorated
crown firmly on
wire frame*

Fig.266

Yugoslavian

*Pill box in felt decorated
with gold coin (with or
without veil)*

Fig.267

Plate 10.   Edwardian Costume

PROPERTIES

The illusion of most small "props", such as are used by dancers, is largely created by the use of wire, felt, cardboard, etc.

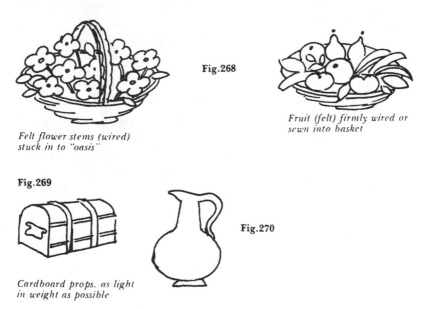

Fig.268

Felt flower stems (wired) stuck in to "oasis"

Fruit (felt) firmly wired or sewn into basket

Fig.269

Fig.270

Cardboard props, as light in weight as possible

Whenever possible, "real life" properties such as peasant baskets, tambourines, fans, etc., can be used. However, many are too heavy or awkward to be manageable, especially if they are to be actually carried whilst dancing.

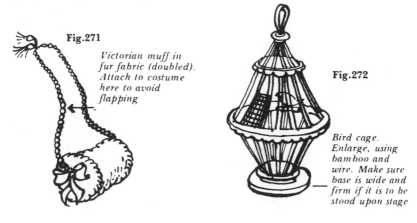

Fig.271

Victorian muff in fur fabric (doubled). Attach to costume here to avoid flapping

Fig.272

Bird cage. Enlarge, using bamboo and wire. Make sure base is wide and firm if it is to be stood upon stage

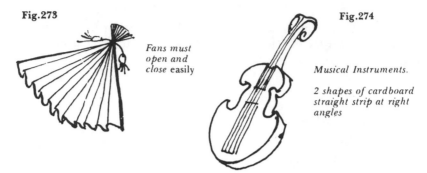

Fig.273

*Fans must
open and
close* easily

Fig.274

Musical Instruments.

*2 shapes of cardboard
straight strip at right
angles*

Whenever there is any doubt about the weight of props, use a light cardboard mock to imitate the real object. Many musical instruments such as violins, lutes, etc., would in any case be too precious to risk on stage, and models of these are better as a rule. When making such properties, simplify the detail and magnify the scale slightly so that the audience can "read" immediately what the model represents the moment it appears and is not left in any doubt, which is distracting.

Care should be taken with properties for national costumes that such items as peasant baskets for fish or fruit, etc., are authentic and really do derive from the specific country. There are many variations and anyone who has visited such countries would quickly spot a mistake or inaccuracy.

Fig.275

*Flower garland for national and
some character dances. Stick the
artificial flowers into the plaited
wire as and where desired. Secure
them with gardeners' wire "tie-
twists".*

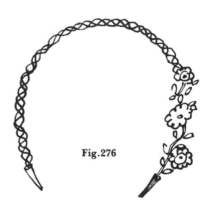

Fig.276

*Use many strands of plaited wire,
fastening ends together with
binding tape to be smooth to the
hands.*

Similarly heraldry — spears, bows and arrows, armour, etc., must be correct and true to the period they depict. Splendid shields, helmets, breast-plates, etc., can be made from cardboard, aluminium kitchen foil, felt, etc., and chainmail can be knitted from dish cloth yarn.

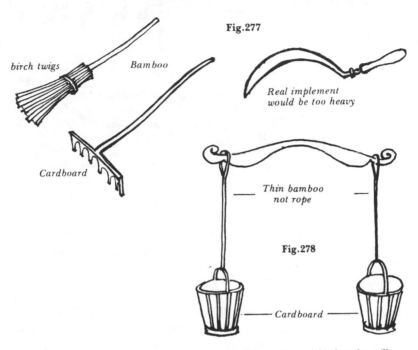

Fig.277

birch twigs   Bamboo

Real implement
would be too heavy

Cardboard

Thin bamboo
not rope

Fig.278

—— Cardboard ——

Cardboard yoke and buckets for milk-
maid, and some National dances, e.g.
Danish.

Many national folk dances have special typical properties such as the Czechoslovakian "ribbon dance", the Russian handkerchief, the Danish yoke and milk bucket, the Spanish fan and castanets. These objects must be carefully made and clearly seen. Make sure they are well-attached when not actually in use. It is not enough for a handkerchief or ribbon, which is to be produced halfway through a performance, to be pushed into a pocket; it will undoubtedly fall out. One corner or end must have a firm press-stud fastening it into the top of the pocket or belt or wherever desired.

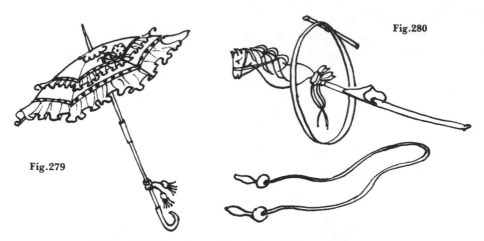

Fig.280

Fig.279

The "real thing" can be used here, if available, as they are all light objects.

It is easy to make the parasol from a child's toy one. Extend the handle and decorate with lace and frill or fringe.

Often some part of the costume needs to be either removed or put on during the dance, such as a cloak, shawl, veil, drape, etc. Special care is needed here to make sure this is easy and quick to manage. Frequently, only one hand is available for this manoeuvre and skill and practice are needed to overcome this difficulty. Taking off is easier than putting on, and very large press-studs or "velcro" on shoulders of capes, etc., may solve many problems. Removable hats and head-dresses must be secured in this case by elastic, both under the chin and beneath the hair at the back, instead of the usual wire-frame method. Putting on is far more difficult and it is only to be hoped that the choreographer can allow this act to be incorporated in his planned movement, to give his dancer a chance to execute this tricky affair, so often involving both hands. Huge hooks and eyes and press-studs are all important aids.

Real flowers and plants are never used on stage. They cannot stand the heat from the lights and are far too unreliable and usually too small to be seen effectively. Excellent artificial ones can now be bought but avoid the small ones. They can also be made of felt. Stems of wire can be covered with machined strips of felt.

Plate 11.   Brazilian National Costume

CLASSICAL TUTU

Fig.281

The Tutu is made in three main sections — Bodice, Basque, and Frilled Briefs. (See Fig.281).

It is very important, when fitting that all 3 sections are tried on together at the same time. Cut them first in lining cotton. Great care must be taken that the lower edge of the basque (where the top frill joins the tutu) is absolutely parallel to the floor — otherwise the result will be a "tilting tutu".

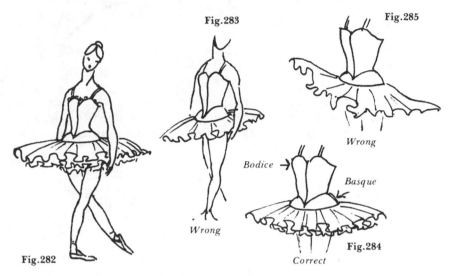

Fig.283

Fig.285

Wrong

Bodice →

Basque

Wrong

Fig.284

Fig.282

Correct

The **Basque** is made first.

Make well-fitting belt in 1″ wide white petersham — not boned.

Cut basic basque shape in paper, and adjust to fit (by trial and error). Then cut in lining cotton, vylene or Victoria Lawn,

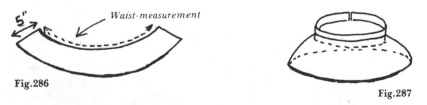

5″

Waist-measurement

Fig.286

Fig.287

Pin inner curve on to petersham. The result must be smooth and flat. It is sometimes necessary to make tiny darts at the top of the basque.

Base for Frilled Briefs.

Cut in 2 pieces, seams at centres front and back.

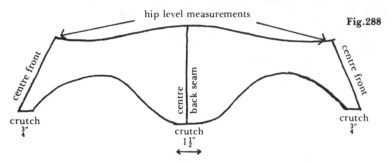

Fig.288

Try out the shape in lining cotton and fit *with* basque and bodice. Make sure the leg-holes are cut high at the sides, curved in at the front, and that they *cover* the buttock muscles at the back. Fit with pins.

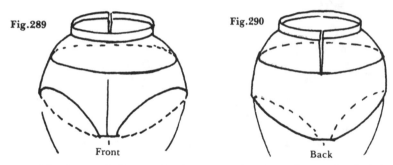

Fig.289   Fig.290

Front   Back

Mark carefully on the basque, the line where the briefs and basque will meet when finished. (This is the line of the top frill.) *Before* continuing with the basque and briefs, cut out the **Bodice** in lining cotton.

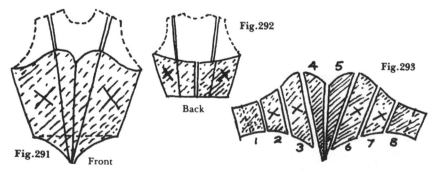

Fig.291   Front   Back   Fig.292   Fig.293

Cut the bodice in 8 pieces, in lining cotton, from the leotard pattern, as shown on previous page. Pieces 2, 3, 6 and 7 (marked X on fig 293) are cut on the cross of the fabric, the other pieces on the straight.

Child's tutu (up to about 10 years, before the bust develops) has 4 pieces, and is also based on the leotard.

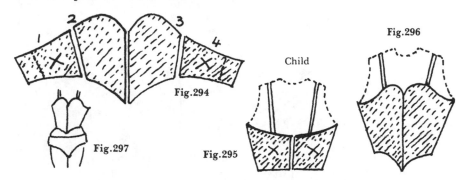

Fig.294

Child

Fig.296

Fig.297

Fig.295

Allow 1″ extra for the seams all round each piece. Fit all together with pins, and adjust. Also pin on the shoulder elastics. When a perfect fit has been achieved, draw carefully between all the pins each side of all the seams. The pins can then be removed, and the pieces separated.

Using these lining fabric pieces as the pattern, pin them on to, and cut out top fabric, in poult or satin for the bodice and basque, and doubled nylon net (in the required colour) for the briefs. Pin all the pieces together again (using the two fabrics as one) and fit all again to check accuracy.
Now separate the three sections.
Seam the Basque on to the petersham, and all the bodice seams.
The cotton lining is not retained inside the briefs, but the frill guide lines are carefully drawn on this lining, and then traced through on to the nylon net.

Fig.298

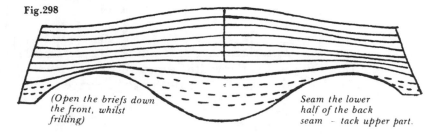

(Open the briefs down the front, whilst frilling)

Seam the lower half of the back seam - tack upper part.

Finishing Briefs.

Edge the legs with pleated, doubled 1″ wide nylon net.

Place, with frilling upwards to edge of leg, and tack. Then face with bias binding, machine stitching over tacking, and then turn to inside and stitch again.

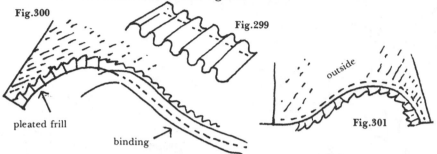

Fig.300

Fig.299

Fig.301

outside

pleated frill

binding

Frills. The number of frills, and the width of the top frill depends upon the height of dancer.
E.G. For Dancer (10 frills) 5′ 4″ tall needs   15″ wide top frill

. .	. .	. .	. .	5′ . .	. . 12″ . . . . . .
. .	. .	. .	. .	or 7 yrs old . .	. . 7″ . . . . . .
. .	. .	. .	. .	9 . .	. . 9″ . . . . . .

Frills.

The more slender the dancer, the less width is needed in the top frill — a heavier dancer needs a wider frill. A short stocky dancer needs a wider frill than is expected for her height.

Frills are made of 54″ wide nylon net, usually sold folded lengthwise, and are cut thus: —

Fig.302

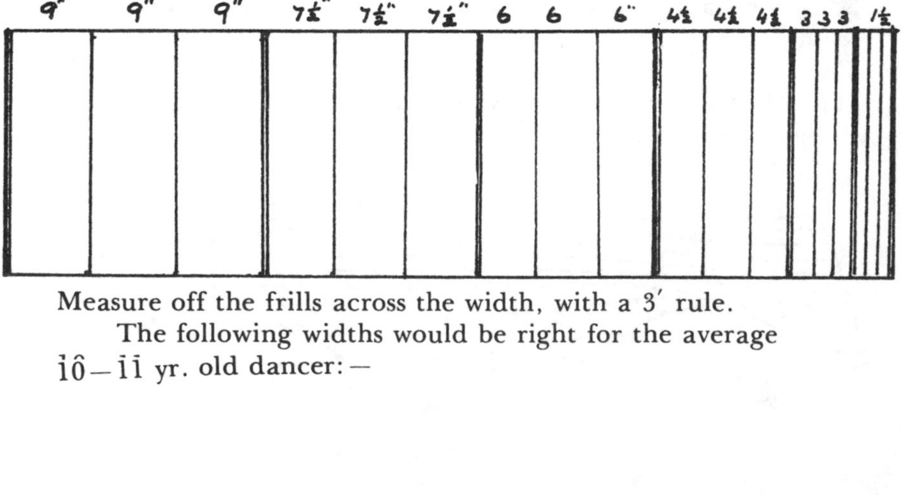

9″	9″	9″	7½″	7½″	7½″	6	6	6″	4½	4½	4½	3 3 3	1½

Measure off the frills across the width, with a 3′ rule.

The following widths would be right for the average $1\hat{0}-1\bar{1}$ yr. old dancer: —

Lowest frill $1\frac{1}{2}''$ wide, and 3 widths of net long

next $3''$ ..   ..

            $4\frac{1}{2}''$ ..   ..

            $6''$ ..   ..

            $7''$ ..   ..

            $9''$ ..   ..

            $10''$ ..   ..

Top frill $11''$ ..   ..

Even in adult sizes, do not put more than 10 frills, but make a bigger "jump" between frill widths: —

$3\frac{1}{2}''$, $5''$, $7\frac{1}{2}''$, $9\frac{1}{2}''$, $11''$, $12''$, $13''$, $14''$ and $15''$.

If any frill is more than $12''$ wide, then these must have 4 widths of net instead of 3.

Using the largest size machine stitch, gather up the 3 widths of each frill, starting with the narrowest $1\frac{1}{2}''$ one, and arrange this on the lowest continuous line on the briefs, frilled edge lying downwards.

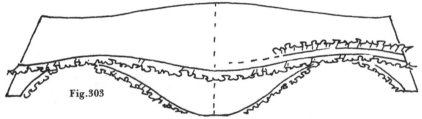

Fig.303

Place the 3" frill on the next line, the frilled edge lying upwards. Place 3rd. frill on the 3rd. line, lying downwards. Place 4th. frill on the 4th line, lying upwards.

Continue thus to top-most frill *but one* — leave this till later.

Fig.304

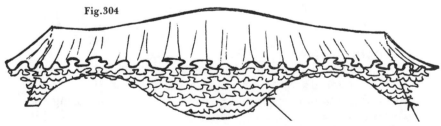

Fill in gaps below lowest frill with tiny doubled 1" frill.

Turn all the frills in and sew up the centre front seam. (It will be very tight, but it is just possible to machine seam.)
All frills will be crammed inside.
Seam up crutch-seam securely.

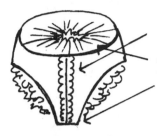

Fig.305

Turn all the frills in and sew up the centre front seam. (It will be very tight, but it is just possible to machine seam).
All frills will be crammed inside.
Seam up crutch seam securely.

Turn the right way out and release the tacking at the top of the centre back seam.

Now arrange the top frill by hand, so that frill lies *downwards*, free ends of frill at centre back.
Sew these free ends together at the outer edge only.
Finish the raw-edges of the crutch seam by hemming them down by hand.

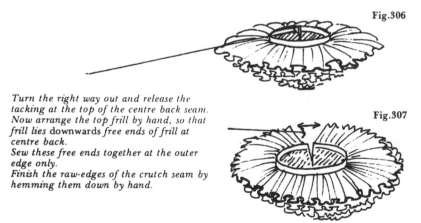

Fig.306

Turn the right way out and release the tacking at the top of the centre back seam.
Now arrange the top frill by hand, so that frill lies downwards *free ends of frill at centre back.*
Sew these free ends together at the outer edge only.
Finish the raw-edges of the crutch seam by hemming them down by hand.

Fig.307

To Finish Basque.

When the fit is obtained in cotton, and the lower edge carefully marked, use this piece as a pattern and pin it to the top fabric — poult or satin. Cut round it, and then using the two fabrics as one, attach it to the petersham waist band. Fit again before machining, making sure the fit is perfect.

Piping.

Cut long strips of top material (poult, satin etc.) 1″ wide, fold lengthwise, enclosing thinnish white string from a new ball. Machine in place with zipper foot. Make about $3\frac{1}{2}$ yds. Tack the piping along line, raw edges of piping *downwards*. Machinestitch on, the string lying on the line.

Turn in the lowest edge of the basque below the line, so that the string is at the very edge.

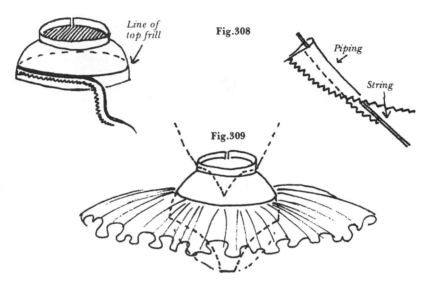

Assemble BRIEFS to BASQUE by hand, back-stitching through the piping and the net together, very firmly.
N.B. This stage may be done later, when the bodice has been attached to the basque.

Finishing Bodice.

Prepare seams, on the wrong side, to take the boning. (This is unnecessary on a child's tutu, up to about 11 years.) On the centre front seam, open the edges and press flat. Lay pieces of white tape or seam-binding over the centre seam, and hem them on to the opened seam edges — do not allow the stitches to penetrate to the right side of the bodice.

At side, and half-back seams (also pressed open) make an extra line of stitching $\frac{1}{3}″$ nearer to the raw edges, on the edge pressed towards the centre back.

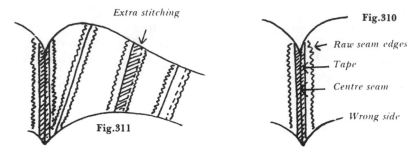

Extra stitching

Fig.310

← *Raw seam edges*

Tape

Centre seam

Wrong side

Fig.311

Tack piping on the marked fitting lines of the bodice top.

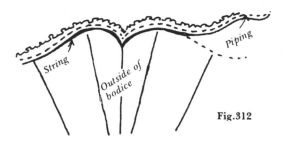

String

Outside of bodice

Piping

Fig.312

Insert the boning (use $\frac{1}{4}''$ wide crinoline wire) cut with pliers to the length required at centre, side and half back-seams. Bind each end of bones with sellotape to prevent the material being torn. The bones will slide easily into position.

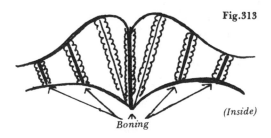

Fig.313

(Inside)

Boning

Now pipe all round the lower bodice edge on the marked fitting line, as at the bodice top, turning to the inside and slip-stitching on to the lining, taking care not to let stitches penetrate to the right side.

Add pleated, doubled nylon-net frill, $1'' - 1\frac{1}{2}''$ wide when finished, on top of the piping at the bodice top — so that frill (doubled) edge lies downwards.

$1 - 1\frac{1}{2}''$ doubled

Fig.314

Finally the top raw edges are faced with bias binding. Tack over the pleated frill, then machine through all thichnesses — facing, frill, piping and bodice top. Turn all to the inside, and slip-stitch down on to the lining as at the lower edge. Trim seams and raw edges as necessary.

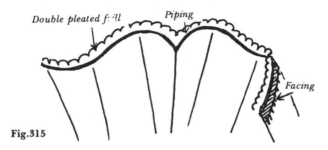

Double pleated frill   Piping

Facing

Fig.315

Assembly.

Fit the basque on. Place the bodice over it. The bases of the side seams lie over the petersham band and basque stitching, pulling tight and flat across the front.

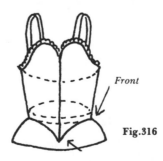

Front

Fig.316

Front point will fall to near the lower edge of the basque.

The base of the bodice will fall over the petersham at the back.

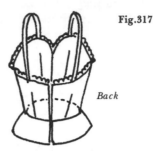

Fig.317

Back

Fit the parts in this position with pins, using narrow pink flat elastic for shoulders.

Fit *with* the briefs, making sure all 3 parts fit together.

Remove the briefs, and stitch the bodice and basque together with zipper foot, so that the stitches lie in the groove of the piping.

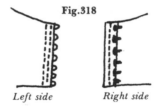

Fig.318

Left side   *Right side*

Fasten down the centre back, with "hook and eye strip", bought at any haberdashery.

Make the closure absolutely "edge-to-edge".

Fig.319   Fig.320

Now pin the frilled briefs on to the basque, matching the centre front seams, and easing in to fit the lower edge of the basque.

Back-stitch by hand neatly between piping and basque, and through the top raw edge of the briefs, *very* firmly, with doubled thread.

Attach a small piece of tape across the outside of the crutch seam, for hanging the tutu up (always upside down) on a hook, and for carrying about.

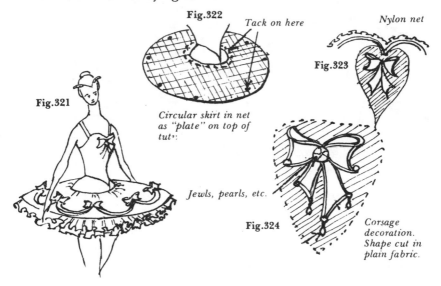

Fig.322

Tack on here

Nylon net

Fig.323

Fig.321

Circular skirt in net as "plate" on top of tutu.

Jewls, pearls, etc.

Fig.324

Corsage decoration. Shape cut in plain fabric.

Variations and Decorations for the Classical Tutu.

A decorated top frill is a charming addition to a classical tutu.

If the decoration is extremely simple, such as a band of ribband as in Fig.326, it is best to add this to the top frill before it is gathered up, and then proceed to fit it on in the usual way.

If, however, a more elaborate or delicate adornment is needed, this should be added to an extra top frill which is cut like a circular skirt (on Pages 34 and 35 Figs.114-116) and which lies upon the finished tutu like a "plate" (Figs.322 and 325). It must be fully decorated before being lightly tacked on to the tutu, both at the join of top frill to basque and also at six to eight points near outer edge, and through two or three layers of frilling beneath.

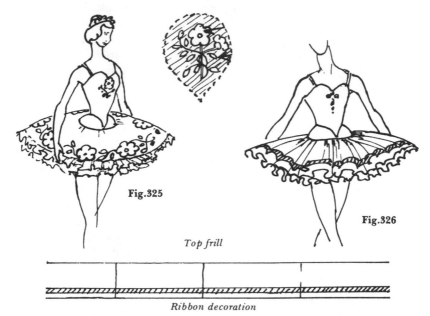

Fig.325

Fig.326

Top frill

Ribbon decoration

The choice of decoration (and the extent) is governed by the strength of the tutu. Only extremely light fabrics must be used as otherwise the weight will produce a "depressed, sagging" tutu which must at all costs be avoided.

Bows, used as described (on Page 66 Figs.196-199), combined with ribbon strip, slightly gathered along one edge to form large "scallops", make a simple and attractive decoration (Fig.321). The accompanying bow on the corsage is not made in this way, however, as it must lie flat, but from fabrics (matching ribband colour) cut out with pinking shears and held into position on the piece of nylon net with Russia braid (Fig.323). Jewels and pearls are added as desired.

"Top Plate" and corsage decorations made in this way and lightly tacked on to the tutu can easily be removed if the character and use of the garment is to be changed.

The floral decoration (Fig.325) is made in exactly the same way — see also "Decorations on Net" for other skirts (Figs.205-207 on Pages 68 and 69). At all times, see that all ornaments are feather-light in weight. A charming combination is of rose flowers, silver lurex leaves and stems, etc., with silver Russia braid; or primrose flowers, gold lurex and gold braid.

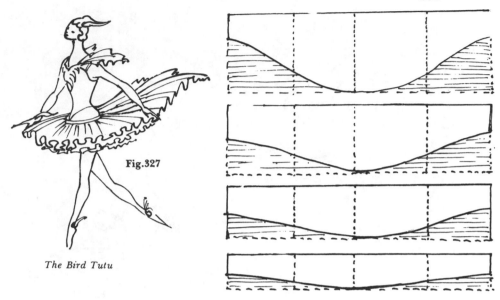

Fig.327

The Bird Tutu

Fig.328   *Four top frills*

Tutus may be adapted for many kinds of character and demi-character work, and can have many uses other than the purely classical. They can be used wherever the movement is essentially balletic. They can even be used in a light-hearted way for musical comedy in circus scenes, etc! The following examples give only a fraction of their many uses: —

The Bird Tutu

Here, the frills are cut wide at the back and a little narrower than usual at the front. The four to six top frills must be cut much too wide and the front edges cut back, see Fig.328). Synthetic shoulder "feathers" of nylon net can be made by gathering half or one width of net of the same shape (though much smaller) as the top frill. Real feathers in the head-dress and possibly at wrist and ankles as well, complete the costume. These are mounted on flesh coloured elastic "garters" (Fig.327).

Fig.329

Fig.330

Fig.331

Fig.332

*Spanish tutu variation
from Don Quixote*

Variations with sleeves (sometimes used for "Aurora", etc.) usually have "built up" bodices (see Fig.329 and 330).

The sleeves are cut like wide national sleeves (Fig.53, 55) and should be made of very soft flowing material such as chiffon or nylon chiffon, and sufficiently transparent to show armline beneath.

Sometimes "puff" sleeves are worn completely free from the bodice and appear like garters — the very soft material being gathered into pink elastic at upper and lower edges (Fig.331).

Fig.333

*Spanish Tutu Variation
From De
Falla's music*

*"National" —
like tutu from
"Coppelia"*

Fig.334

Some tutus take on an almost "peasant national" aspect, especially noticeable in the bodice decorations (Figs.332, 333 and 334). The bodice from the Coppelia type tutu has no prolonged point and is surmounted by a soft chiffon blouse-like top, gathered into a "scoop" neckline. The frills at the shoulders should be of nylon net, decorated with two bands of ribband as are the three flounces which are added to the top frill of the tutu.

Plate 12.   Romantic Tutu, style of Degas drawings

THE ROMANTIC TUTU

Fig.335

The simple romantic tutu consists of the same basic bodice as the classical, usually without the point at the waistline.

The basque differs only in that it is completely covered by the skirt frills, instead of being exposed above them.

It is therefore made of the foundation material only.

.Finish with piping, fastenings on edge frilling and facings, as before

The 8 pieces are fitted and assembled exactly as for the classical tutu. (Without the point at centre front.)
Note. Child's bodice has only 4 pieces, as before.

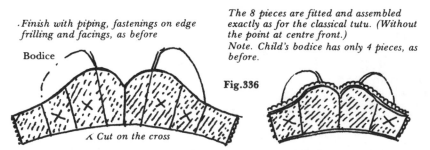

Fig.336

Bodice

∧ Cut on the cross

Make *petersham band* at waist, and fit the basque exactly as before. On this, mark out with 4 lines each 1″ apart, so that the top line is only ½″ from the top edge, and lies on the petersham.

The skirts consist of 4 layers of nylon net. Each layer of 3 widths of nylon net, 54″ wide. Start with the lowest, the length of which is that from the lowest line to mid-calf.

The 2nd frill is cut 1″ longer, and is gathered on to the 2nd line. The 3rd frill is cut 2″ longer, and is gathered on to the 3rd line. The top frill is cut 3″ longer, and is gathered on to the top line. the top frill will need 4 widths.

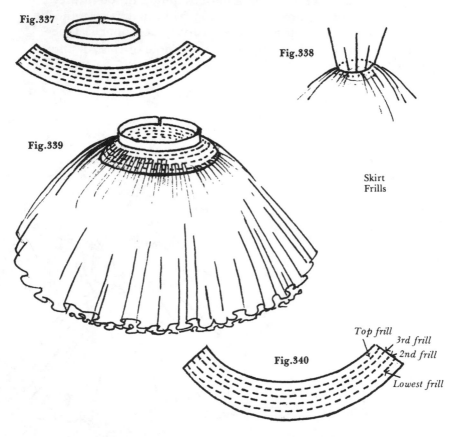

Fig.337

Fig.338

Fig.339

Skirt
Frills

Top frill
3rd frill
2nd frill

Fig.340

Lowest frill

Assemble bodice over the skirts at the petersham band, by turning the raw edges of the bodice under, and covering the join of the top frill with this.

The uses of costumes based on the romantic tutu are numberless. They vary from the type used in the great classical ballets, which are the simplest form of this costume, to the most exuberant and ornate national or peasant costume.

All are constructed fundamentally as described above — all decorations being added to each part before it is assembled. The colour of the costume, the detail and variety of the ornament explain the character and mood of the tutu. Dreamy soft translucency gives the "feel" of "Swan Lake" or "Sylphides", while floral garlands or ornate corsage that of the Napoli variations (Fig.344).

Many mid-European national costumes, although they will have an opaque material for top frill (or skirt), should be thought of basically as a romantic tutu. The Coppelia type costumes (Figs.345 and 346) are an example of this, despite their delicate top skirt.

"Swan Lake" type

Fig.341
"Les Sylphides" type

The "dropped" waistline on a romantic tutu gives an Edwardian flavour, as was so well-established with the "Two Pigeons" designs (Fig.348) and, similarly, the "Degas" type design (Fig.347) shown here. The bodice is prolonged over the top frills and stitched down carefully at hip level through the layers of net. If a very deep drop is needed, it is easier to construct the skirt as described under "National Petticoats" (Figs.144-146) in which case the bodice is drawn down and attached over the join of the top frill to the underlying circular skirt.

Fig.342

"La Sylphide" type

Fig.343

"La Fille Mal Grandée" type

Fig.344

"Napoli variation" type

Fig.345

*Slightly dropped
waist line*

Fig.346

"Coppelia" type

If very delicate decorations are needed on the skirt itself
— which might well be lost in the folds of the top frill — it is
best to add a single net circular skirt which has been
previously decorated as desired (Figs.345 and 349). The net of
this does not show but it makes sure that all the ornament
remain on the surface of the tutu skirt.

Fig.347

*Degas type
(dropped waist line)*

Fig.348

*"Two pigeons" type
(dropped waist line)*

Fig.349

Victorian Romantic

*Top "plate"
decorated*

Plate 13.   Child's Costume for "Snow-White"

MEN'S CLASSICAL COSTUME

Although there is considerable variation, these usually consist of some form of tunic worn over skin-fitting tights.

Velvet, or similar fabric, is often used for the tunics and a good fit must be obtained from the leotard pattern described in Section 1. Perfect fit is essential as is also great freedom for strong movements. Invisible insertion of matching elastic at various points such as side seams can help considerably.

The examples shown here are a few of the typical variations. As before mentioned, the soft loose (but well-cut) shirt is much used, especially in romantic work. It is often combined with waistcoat-like tunics as in Figs.350 and 355).

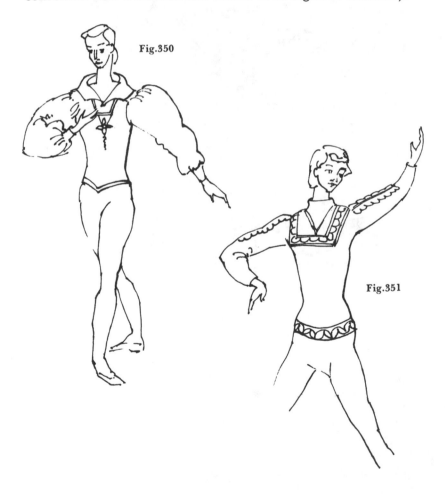

Fig.350

Fig.351

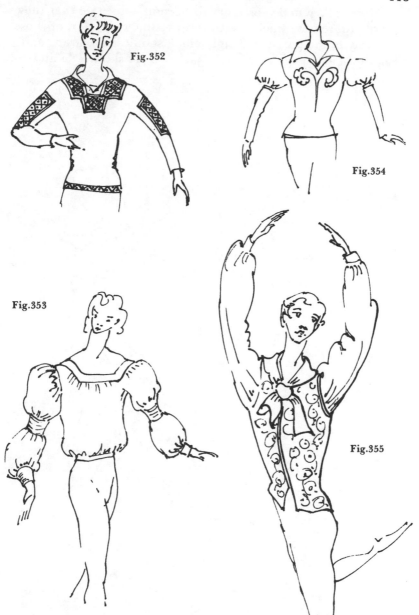

Fig.352

Fig.354

Fig.353

Fig.355

Touches of "period" can be shown in sleeve and edge decorations, as in Figs.351, 353 and 354; an extension of the "slashed" sleeve idea is shown in Fig.356.

Never allow male costumes to become so ornate that they hide the movement line — with the possible exception of those for purely mime parts. A Kingly cloak should have grace and elegance, and a page's elaborate jacket must show style and design.

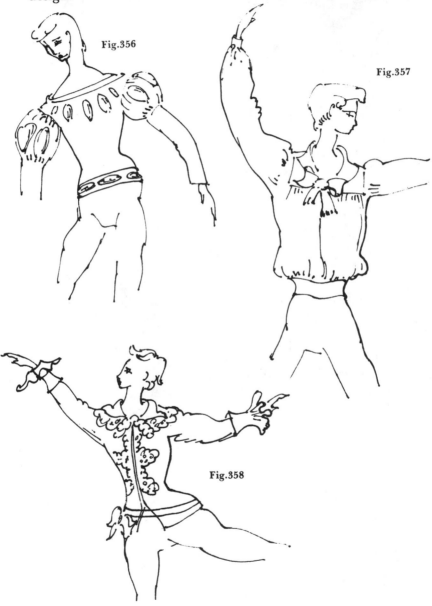

Fig.356

Fig.357

Fig.358

GREEK DANCE COSTUME

Fig.360

Fig.361

Ceres

Mountain Mist

Fig.362

The costumes used for "Greek" dance today are far removed from those of the great Hellenic period from which they originate. However, what has been preserved of the "Chiton", "Peoplos" and "Heimation" of ancient times should be carefully shown in today's version of these classic designs.

The original garments were made almost without seams from straight lengths of material, the top edge being "turned over" to give the "flounce" effect so often seen on the Greek vase designs.

Fig.363

Lunaria (Moon
Flower called
"Honesty")

Fig.364

Wood-nymph

Fig.365

Fig.366

Philomel

From these ancient designs a great sense of movement and
freedom comes to us to this very day, and this is essentially
what must be seen and felt in our own "Greek" dance
costume. For this purpose, extremely light diaphanous
materials such as chiffon or georgette or nylon or crystal nylon
chiffon are used, always over a well-fitted leotard. Straight
pieces of fabric are used, gathered to the neck of the leotard
at front and back. The neck may need to be slightly "scooped"
out at the centre (Fig.368). The sides are left almost unseamed
except for a few inches from underarm to waist. The seams
below this being left open.

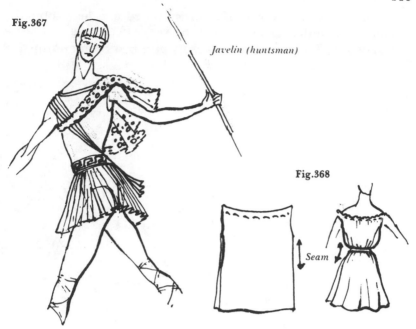

Fig.367

Javelin (huntsman)

Fig.368

Seam

The short tunic or "chiton" is most usually worn, often held in to the waist with a cord. The illusion of the "turned over" top part of the garment is given by adding an extra short flounce of the same material, also gathered to the same neckline and usually cut a little higher in front than at the back (Fig.360, 371).

For all lyrical Greek work, the dancer should appear to be dressed simply in a leotard (which must fit perfectly) with the merest "whiff" of classical drapery over it.

More opaque materials, however, can be used for stoic and athletic Greek dance such as the Discus and Javelin movements, huntsmen, etc. These dances are used for male and female dancers, and fabrics such as gold and silver lurex, fur fabric and leather are used. Men's legs may be cross-gartered and feet often sandalled (Fig.367).

Slightly heavier materials of a darker colour may be used for Tragedy, and such nature subjects as storm, wind, winter, etc., dictate their own demands for colour and material.

At all times, much should be made of the folds of the material which greatly emphasise the movement and mood of the dance and music.

Sometimes, an all-over pattern is needed and here spotted or patterned chiffon or muslin can be very effective, as in the leaf design in Fig.364 for the wood-nymph and the dewdrop design for Eos, goddess of dew (Fig.370).

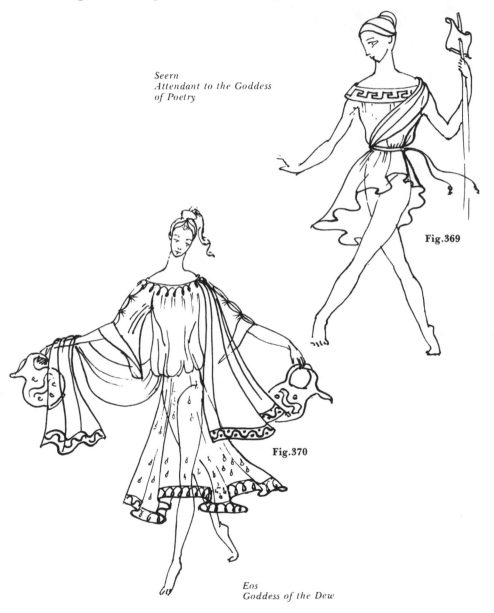

Seern
Attendant to the Goddess
of Poetry

Fig.369

Fig.370

Eos
Goddess of the Dew

Patterns, border designs and other decorations must be in keeping with the dance theme yet should be kept as formal as possible. The Greek key pattern predominates and formalised "nature" designs — leaves, shells, flowers, birds, etc., all take their place (Fig.372).

Complete freedom must be the over-riding impression, however. Bare feet and loose (though well-groomed) hair exemplify this. Hair should be secured away from the face by a simple head-dress consisting of bands across the forehead and round the head, in traditional Greek style. The hair may then be allowed to fall freely and loosely behind this from the back of the head.

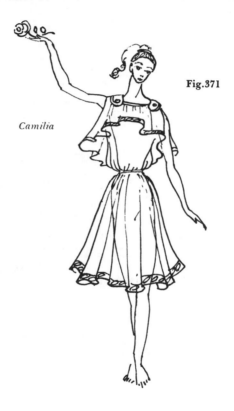

Camilia

Fig.371

Note: For instructions for making Greek Practice Tunic, see Page 140.

Fig.372

*Border designs suitable for Greek costumes. See Section 6 for
instructions on making.*

Group Work Costumes

Making costumes for groups of dancers can be a delightful affair.

Although it is for the designer to create the "atmosphere" of the costumes, both as the group and individuals, it is the costumier's task to see that the designs are adapted to each dancer's needs so that each one appears to perfection, both in his or her own right and as part of the group.

Nearly every costume in the group has some variation within the theme. Often each dancer is differently costumed. However, if this is so, there will always be a unifying factor throughout, be it shape, colour, period, national detail or ornament. When the costumes vary very considerably, the dressmaker must make sure that whatever factor or detail *is* uniform to all the group, it is *exactly* uniform, as this forms the essential "tying together" detail.

Fig.373

Basic Edwardian shapes uniform but colours and details different.

Nothing looks worse than a set of mass-produced costumes which barely, if ever, fit any member of the cast. Each must be made separately, with careful perfection for every individual dancer, as if it were intended for the main soloist. Only then does the group look really well-costumed.

Costumes identical except for colours of leaf details.

Fig.374

Uniform shape and colours of costumes. Embroidery details different.

Fig.375

Man's Costume, Cossack Dancers

Plate 14.   Hungarian National Costume for a child

PACKING AND TRAVELLING WITH COSTUMES

There can, unfortunately, be a vast difference in appearance of costumes between that in which they leave the costumier and that in which they are seen on stage!

A little trouble taken to preserve their pristine crispness is well worthwhile.

These days we owe a great deal to the help given by the long suffering "plastic bag" and costumes (on hangers) in such bags travel extremely well, even if fairly tightly crushed together. To transport them by car or van, all that is necessary is to cover them with long "cleaners" bags and lay them flat in the car boot or on the seat or van floor — always putting the heaviest and toughest beneath, the most delicate on top.

However, if no such transport is available, the old-fashioned wicker "skip" is all that is necessary and holds a tremendous amount. The only snag being that it takes two strong people to carry it. The same must be said for trunks. The most manageable hold-alls are large light suitcases and, if these are used, simple folding will be needed.

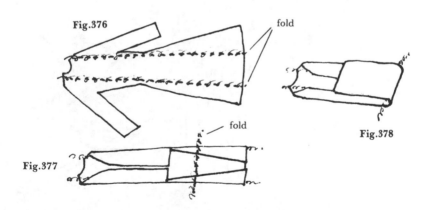

Fig.376

fold

Fig.378

fold

Fig.377

1. Lay the costume out flat, full-length (Fig.376) and fold on dotted lines, placing tissue paper, wadding or even newspaper rolls along the lines, and fold costume over these (Fig.377).

2. If necessary, fold again across garment as well (Fig.378).

It is helpful to pack like articles in the same container, eg. have one case for *all* footwear, another for head-dresses, another for properties and, of course, a separate one for make-up. The largest case being left for the costumes themselves.

A great boon on arrival at the dressing room is to have a costume stand. Often this is there already but it is worthwhile to find this out beforehand and, if none is available, to procure a portable one. This can be made by any carpenter for little cost and consists of three wooden or steel poles with two sets of crossed wooden blocks to support the two uprights at the base (Fig.379), not unlike a pair of high jump stands. The uprights fit into prepared sockets in the base and the cross-bar is slotted through the uprights near the top. A set of 10-20 costumes is extremely heavy so the uprights, bases and cross-bar must all be really strong.

When packing car or van, always see that the stand is available first so that it can be erected before the costumes are unloaded. In this way, they can be placed immediately on to it with the minimum risk of crushing.

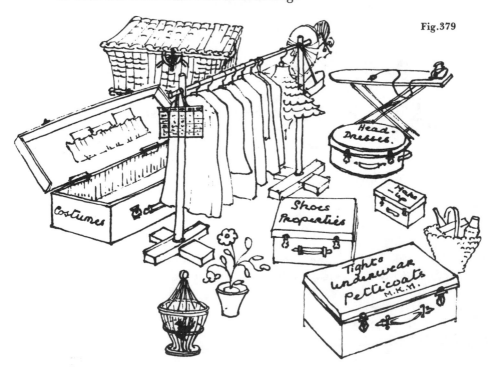

Fig.379

A carefully made out costume and accessory list can be a great asset — a chart showing every requirement for each costume. The anxiety of the dresser to remember every detail is thereby much reduced (Fig.380). In this way, every item can be checked both before travelling and when unpacking.

If possible, allow time on arrival for the inevitable "stitch" to be applied, and a touch here and there with an iron is well worth the extra bother of transporting a travelling electric iron and board.

Always arrive in plenty of time!

Dance	Costume	Head-dress	Foot-wear	Underwear	Hosiery	Props
Ballet	white tutu	classical hair style pearl coronet	pink points	pink briefs	pink tights	
Character	Victorian	Lace and ribband Victorian with Veil	black points	national petticoat and drawers	white tights	fan
National	Portuguese	Victorian hair style Mimosa wreath, Head-scarf (2)	black leather flats	national petticoat and drawers	black tights	fish basket and net (2)
Greek	White hunting greek, fur ½ cape & purple drape	hair tight back into high tail. Gold leaf classical wreath		white briefs		spear
Modern	Draped Red leotard	high bun		white briefs	Red footless tights	
Group	Edwardian Muslin, primrose	Hair looped up to high Veil at back primrose bow	black points	small petticoat national drawers	black tights	blossom spray
TOTAL NUMBERS	6	6	3	5	4	5

Examples of costume chart. Fig.380

Plate 15. Victorian Costume for "The Bride of Lammermuir"

PRACTICE TIGHTS (Knitted) Fig.381

Knitted in 3 ply wool, preferably a mixture of wool and nylon.

Materials: 1 pr. No. 11 Knitting needles.

         1 pr. No. 12   . .   . .

         7 ozs. or 8 x 25 gram balls.

Measurements, To fit 34/35″ hips.

        and To fit 36/37″ hips.

         Length from waist to crutch at front $11\frac{1}{2}$″.

Tension: 8 sts. = 1″ on No. 11 needles.

N.B. Instructions for larger size given in brackets thus ( ).

Right leg. With No. 12 needles, cast on 64 (68) sts. and work $2\frac{1}{2}$″ in k.1, p.1 rib. for both sizes. Change to No. 11 needles and stocking-stitch, increasing at each end of next and every following 16th (14th) row until there are 94 (104) sts. Work straight until inside leg seam is of required length.

Now increase at each end of every row until there are 126 (136) sts. Then decrease at each end of next and every following 3rd row until 110 (124) sts. remain.

Now keep front edge straight and continue, decreasing at back edge on next and every following 3rd row until 94 (104) sts. remain. Work straight until front edge measures 8 ($8\frac{1}{2}$) in. from start of decreasings, ending with a knit row.

Here shape back: 1st row: p.65 (70) turn and knit back. 3rd row: p.60 (65), turn and knit back. 5th row: p.55 (60) turn and knit back. Continue thus, working 5 sts. less each time. Your last 2 rows will read: p.5, turn and knit back.

Next row purl over all sts.⊕ Change to No. 12 needles and work 2″ in k.1, p.1 rib. Next row, *k.1, sl.1, psso, m.1* repeat from * to * to last stitch. Knit another 1″ in k.1, p.1 rib. Cast off loosely in rib.

Left leg. Work to correspond with right leg, reversing all shapings.

Gusset. With No. 11 needles, cast on 2 sts. and work in st.st., increasing at each end of every alt. row until there are 28 sts. Then decrease at each end of every alt. row, until 2 sts. remain. Cast off.

To Make up. Join front and back seams, then leg seams and insert gusset. Press with a damp cloth. Insert Elastic.

PRACTICE TIGHTS (Knitted)

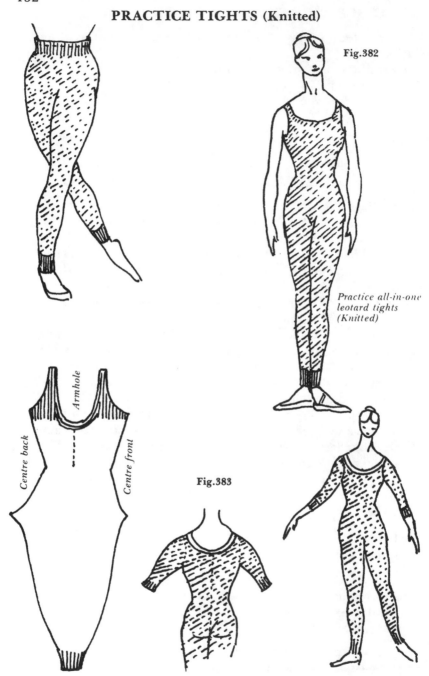

Fig.382

Practice all-in-one
leotard tights
(Knitted)

Centre back

Armhole

Centre front

Fig.383

PRACTICE ALL-IN-ONE LEOTARD — TIGHTS
(Knitted)

Materials: 12 ozs. or 14 x 25 gram balls of 3 ply wool and
nylon mixture.

This useful garment is made in 2 simple pieces — plus
gusset.

Right leg. As for "Practice Tights" to ⊕, after back shaping.
94 stitches. Continue as follows: —
st.st. 15 rows without shaping.
16th row: k.46, make 1 in each of next 2 sts, (47th and 48th),
k.46. Continue in st.st. increasing twice at centre of every 16th
row till there are 100sts. Work another 15 rows st.st.

Arm-hole shaping (at centre of work).
1st row: k.44, k.2 tog., k.1. p.1, k.1. p.1. Place these sts. on a
holder and cont. across 1st. row as follows: —
k.1, p.1, k.1, p.1, k.2 tog., k. remaining 44 sts. to
end.
Put 1st set of stitches on a stitch holder. On 2nd set,
continue as follows: —
2nd row: p. to last 5 sts. p.2 tog., k.1, p.1, k.1.
3rd row: p.1, k.1, p.1, k.2 tog., k. to end.
4th row: p. to last 5 sts., p.2 tog., k.1, p.1, k.1.
Repeat 3rd and 4th row till 40 sts. remain. Continue decreasing
every *knit* row only, just inside the rib, till 32 sts. remain.
St.st. without shaping for $1\frac{1}{2} - 2''$ (keeping k.1, p.1, k.1, p.1.
rib at arm-hole edge). Then k.1, p.1. rib right across all sts, for 4
rows.

Neck Decreasing. (Front and Back alike).
1st row at front edge, cast off 8 stitches rib to end.
2nd row rib to end.
3rd row cast off 8 stitches at centre front edge rib to end.
4th row rib to end.
5th row cast off 8 stitches at centre front edge.
On last 8 sts., rib to required length to reach to top of shoulder,
about 3″. Cast off.
Work 2nd shoulder to correspond, reversing shapings.

Left leg. As right leg, reversing all shapings.

Gussett as for "Tights"

To Make up. Sew up leg seams, inserting gusset, and centre front and back seams. Press carefully.

If sleeves are required, work as above, omitting ribbing around arm-holes.

For short sleeves, work these as for "cross-over", if $\frac{3}{4}$ length sleeves: —

Cast on 64 sts., on No. 12 needles, and rib for 2 inches.

Change to No. 11 needles and continue in st.st., increasing both ends of every 14th row, till there are 68 sts. Then continue as short sleeves.

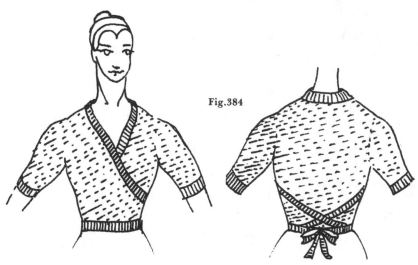

Fig.384

CROSS-OVER (Knitted)

Materials: 4 ozs. or 5 x 25 gram balls 3 ply wool and nylon mixture.

Measurements: 31" bust.

        17" long, shoulder to base.

    and 33" bust, larger size

        17" long.

      Sleeves, inner seam 5".

Tension: 7½ sts. and 10 rows = 1" on No. 10 needles.

N.B. Larger size in brackets ( ).

Back. With No. 12 needles, cast on 94 (104) sts.
Work 1″ in k.2, p.2 rib.
No. 10 needles and st.st., increasing at each end of 7th and
every following 6th row until there are 118 (126) sts.
St.st. without shaping till work measures 10 ins.
Arm-holes. Cast off 5 (6) sts. at beg. of next 2 rows.
Knit 2 tog. at each end of every alternate row until 70 (96) sts.
remain. St.st. without shaping till work measures 17 ins.
Shoulders. Cast off 10 (11) sts. at beg. of next 6 rows.
Cast off.

Fronts.
Left. With No. 12 needles, cast on 72 (78) sts.
1″ of k.2, p.2. rib.
St.st. on No. 10 needles. Increase at side edge on 7th and then
every 6th row 11 times in all. *At the same time* decrease 1 st.
at front edge on next and every following 4th row 22 (20)
times, then continue decreasing at this edge on every 3rd row.

Meanwhile when work measures 10 ins, shape arm-hole by
casting off 5 (6) sts. at beg. of next row, side edge, then k.2
tog. on every alt. row, this edge, 9 times.

Now keep armhole edge straight and continue decreasing
at neck edge on every 3rd row until 30 (33) sts. remain. Work
straight until front matches back, then shape shoulder by
casting off 10 (11) sts. at beg. of next and following 2 alt.
rows, armhole edge.
Right. Work to correspond with left front, reversing shapings.

Bands. With No. 12 needles, cast on 8 sts. and work a strip of
garter-stitch long enough to go up left front, round back of
neck and down right front, when slightly stretched. Sew this
on as you go to ensure a good fit.

Ties (2) With No. 12 needles, cast on 8 sts. and work in garter
stitch for 28 ins. Cast off.

Sleeves. No. 12 needles, cast on 78 sts., and work 1 inch in
k.1, p.1. rib.
No. 10 needles, st.st., increasing at each end of next and every
following 4th row until there are 96 sts.
St.st. without shaping till sleeve measures 5 ins.

Cast off 4 sts. at beg. of next 2 rows, then k.2 tog. at each end of every alternate row until 56 remain, then at each end of every row until 20 sts. remain.

To Make up. Join side seams, leaving a small opening about 1 in. from bottom on right side.
Join shoulder and sleeve seams.
Insert sleeves.
Sew ties to edges of fronts at waist. Press carefully.

CHILD'S CROSS-OVER

Materials: 4 ozs or 4 x 25 gram balls 3 ply wool and nylon
    mixture.
Measurement: Chest 27″, length from shoulder $13\frac{1}{4}$″
    sleeve seam 4″.
Tension: $7\frac{1}{2}$ sts. and 10 rows = 1″ on No. 10 needles.

Back. No. 12 needles, cast on 92 sts., and work $\frac{1}{2}$″ in k.2, p.2 rib.
No. 10 needles, st.st. straight for 7 ins (including rib).
Shape armholes by casting off 4 sts. at beg. of next 2 rows. Then knit 2 tog. at each end of every alt. row till 72 sts remain. St.st. straight till work measures 13 ins., then *shape shoulders* by casting off 9 sts., at beg. of next 6 rows. Cast off.

Fronts.
Left. No. 12 needles, cast on 64 sts., and work $\frac{1}{2}$″ in k.2, p.2 rib.
No. 10 needles, st.st., decreasing at front edge on 5th and every following 4th row until side edge measures 7 ins. Still decreasing at each edge on every 4th row, shape armhole by casting off 4 sts., at beg. of next row, side edge, then knit 2 tog. on every alt. row at this edge 6 times in all. Now keep this edge straight and continue decreasing on every 4th row at each edge until 27 sts., remain. Work straight till front matches back, then shape shoulders by casting off 9 sts. at beg. of next 3 alt. rows, armhole edge.

Right. Work to match left, reversing shapings.

Sleeves. No. 12 needles, cast on 68 sts. and work $\frac{1}{2}$″ in k.2, p.2 rib.

No 10. needles, st.st., incr. at each end of 7th and every
following 4th row until there are 78 sts. Work straight till
sleeve measures 4 ins. Shape top by casting off 4 sts. at beg. of
next 2 rows. Then knit 2 tog. at beg. of every alt. row until 50
sts. remain, then at each end of every row until 24 sts. remain.
Cast off.
Bands. exactly as for adult, but cast on only 6 sts.
Ties.   · ·   · ·   · ·   · · only 26″ long.
Make Up. · ·   · ·   · ·   · ·

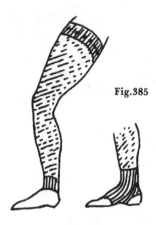

Fig.385

LEG WARMERS (Knitted)

Materials: 6 — 7 x 25 gram balls of 3 ply wool/nylon mixture.
Follow directions for knitted tights till work measures required
leg-length.
k.1, p.1 rib for 2″
Line of holes (k.1, p.1, k.2 tog, make 1)
k.1, p.1 rib for another 1″
Cast off.
Sew up long seam, and elasticise at top.

Leg Warmer — With Feet.

Exactly as above, except that the ribbing at the foot is 3 times
as long.
To make up, leave centre $\frac{1}{3}$″ of the ribbing un-seamed, the
heel projects through this — the lowest $\frac{1}{3}$ encircling insteps.

Plate 16.   Hungarian National Costume

SIMPLE PRACTICE TUNIC

Using leotard pattern, cut back and front alike, without
shaping at sides. Dart slightly at front (optional), and sew ties
of same fabric at sides at waist line, to tie at back, these draw
the tunic in to fit.

Leave side seam un-joined below waist line. Face these edges,
neck and arm-holes with bias binding.

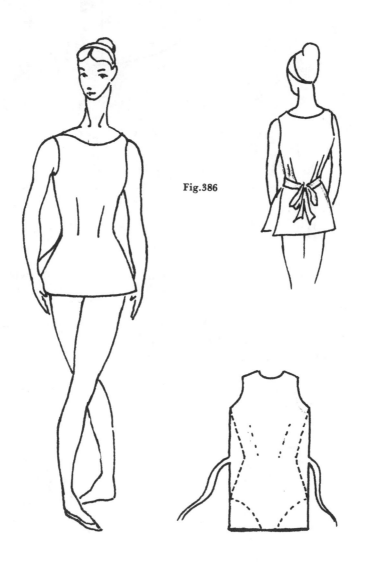

Fig.386

Greek Practice Tunic

To make a simple practice tunic for Greek work

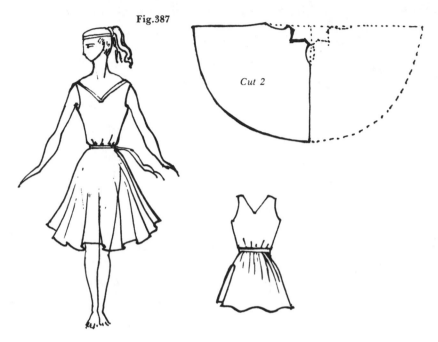

Fig.387

Cut 2

Cut a semi-circle of plain light material, fold into two and cut out V at centre for neck and slight curve at either side for armholes.

Join shoulder seams and side seams from armhole to hip level. Then allow hemmed edges to fall free.

Use bias binding at neck and armholes but leave lower edge to "drop" for a few days before binding this also.

Carefully match the tunic colour for hairband and waist cord and well-fitting briefs.

Plate 17.   Sicilian National Costume

Plate 18.   C19th Italian Costume from Campania

KNITTING — Comparative Needle Sizes

British	USA	French
1	13	9.25
2	11	8.00
3	10½	7.00
4	10	6.00
5	9	5.50
6	8	5.00
7	7	4.75
8	6	4.50
9	5	4.00
10	3	3.25
11	3	3.00
12	1	2.50

Standard Conversion of Inches to Millimetres

Inches	Milli-metres	Inches	Milli-metres	Inches	Milli-metres	Inches	Milli-metres
$\frac{1}{8}$″	3	10″	254	27″	686	44″	1.118
$\frac{1}{4}$″	6	11″	279	28″	711	45″	1.143
$\frac{3}{8}$″	9	12″	305	29″	737	46″	1.168
$\frac{1}{2}$″	13	13″	330	30″	762	47″	1.194
$\frac{5}{8}$″	16	14″	356	31″	787	48″	1.219
$\frac{3}{4}$″	19	15″	381	32″	813	49″	1.245
$\frac{7}{8}$″	22	16″	406	33″	838	50″	1.270
		17″	432	34″	864	51″	1.295
1″	25	18″	457	35″	889	52″	1.321
2″	51	19″	483	36″	914	53″	1.346
3″	76	20″	508	37″	940	54″	1.372
4″	102	21″	533	38″	965		
5″	127	22″	559	39″	991		
6″	152	23″	584	40″	1.016		
7″	178	24″	610	41″	1.041		
8″	203	25″	635	42″	1.067		
9″	229	26″	660	43″	1.092		

Index